Illuminating Selections
from Scripture

LIGHT FOR
MY PATH
for
Teens

Illuminating Selections
from Scripture

LIGHT FOR
MY PATH

for
Teens

BARBOUR
PUBLISHING

Published by Barbour Publishing Inc., P.O. Box 719, Uhrichsville, Ohio 44683, www.barbourbooks.com

Our mission is to publish and distribute inspirational products offering exceptional value and biblical encouragement to the masses.

ecpa Member of the
Evangelical Christian
Publishers Association

Printed in the United States of America.

Contents

Introduction

As a teen, you've got enough stresses in life—you may be worried about that upcoming school event or your next exam. When you're facing so much at once, where do you turn?

That's what *Light for my Path for Teens* is all about. This collection of scriptures, drawn from several popular Bible translations, will sharpen your focus on the *real* issues of life—spiritual matters of the deepest importance. You'll find forty-one relevant topics, each packed with God's ultimate truth. Brief introductions and thought-provoking quotations enhance each section, making this a book to refer to for years to come.

Of course, no book should substitute for daily Bible reading and study. We hope *Light for My Path for Teens* will always point you toward the one Book that *is* truth—the Bible. With God's Word as your guide, you can't go wrong in the life ahead!

Adversity

One of Satan's biggest falsehoods is that the Christian life should be free of adversity. The longer you live, the more you'll realize that adversity is the *rule* in life, not the exception. But don't look at problems as things to be avoided: These are the times that test your character, patience, and faith. Sure, we might suffer grief and pain, but with Christ, we can endure any hardship. Hey, Job lost everything—but he still gave glory to God.

The LORD also will be a refuge for the oppressed, a refuge in times of trouble. And those who know Your name will put their trust in You; for You, LORD, have not forsaken those who seek You.

PSALM 9:9–10 NKJV

When everything
seems to be going against you,
remember that the airplane
takes off against the wind,
not with it.
HENRY FORD

For even Christ did not please himself but, as it is written: "The insults of those who insult you have fallen on me." For everything that was written in the past was written to teach us, so that through endurance and the encouragement of the Scriptures we might have hope.

ROMANS 15:3–4 NIV

Are any among you suffering? They should keep on praying about it. And those who have reason to be thankful should continually sing praises to the Lord.

JAMES 5:13 NLT

Even though I walk through the valley of the shadow of
death, I fear no evil, for You are with me; Your rod and Your
staff, they comfort me.

PSALM 23:4 NASB

"When you pass through the waters, I will be with you; and
through the rivers, they will not overflow you. When you
walk through the fire, you will not be scorched, nor will the
flame burn you."

ISAIAH 43:2 NASB

For the Lord will not reject forever, for if He causes grief,
then He will have compassion according to His abundant
lovingkindness.

LAMENTATIONS 3:31–32 NASB

But rejoice to the extent that you partake of Christ's sufferings, that when His glory is revealed, you may also be glad
with exceeding joy.

1 PETER 4:13 NKJV

For as the sufferings of Christ abound in us, so our consolation also aboundeth by Christ. And whether we be afflicted,
it is for your consolation and salvation, which is effectual
in the enduring of the same sufferings which we also suffer:
or whether we be comforted, it is for your consolation and
salvation. And our hope of you is stedfast, knowing, that as
ye are partakers of the sufferings, so shall ye be also of the
consolation.

2 CORINTHIANS 1:5–7 KJV

Casting all your care upon Him, for He cares for you.

                              1 PETER 5:7 NKJV

"Blessed are those who mourn, for they shall be comforted."

                              MATTHEW 5:4 NKJV

He will swallow up death forever! The Sovereign LORD will wipe away all tears. He will remove forever all insults and mockery against his land and people. The LORD has spoken!

                              ISAIAH 25:8 NLT

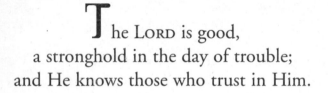

The LORD is good,
a stronghold in the day of trouble;
and He knows those who trust in Him.

NAHUM 1:7 NKJV

If you are reproached for the name of Christ, blessed are you, for the Spirit of glory and of God rests upon you. On their part He is blasphemed, but on your part He is glorified.

                              1 PETER 4:14 NKJV

Record my lament; list my tears on your scroll—are they not in your record? Then my enemies will turn back when I call for help. By this I will know that God is for me.

PSALM 56:8–9 NIV

"Come to Me, all you who labor and are heavy laden, and I will give you rest. Take My yoke upon you and learn from Me, for I am gentle and lowly in heart, and you will find rest for your souls. For My yoke is easy and My burden is light."

MATTHEW 11:28–30 NKJV

For this finds favor, if for the sake of conscience toward God a person bears up under sorrows when suffering unjustly. For what credit is there if, when you sin and are harshly treated, you endure it with patience? But if when you do what is right and suffer for it you patiently endure it, this finds favor with God. For you have been called for this purpose, since Christ also suffered for you, leaving you an example for you to follow in His steps, who committed no sin, nor was any deceit found in His mouth; and while being reviled, He did not revile in return; while suffering, He uttered no threats, but kept entrusting Himself to Him who judges righteously.

1 PETER 2:19–23 NASB

"Do not fear any of those things which you are about to suffer. Indeed, the devil is about to throw some of you into prison, that you may be tested, and you will have tribulation ten days. Be faithful until death, and I will give you the crown of life."

REVELATION 2:10 NKJV

For our light affliction, which is but for a moment, worketh for us a far more exceeding and eternal weight of glory.

2 CORINTHIANS 4:17 KJV

And lest I should be exalted above measure through the abundance of the revelations, there was given to me a thorn in the flesh, the messenger of Satan to buffet me, lest I should be exalted above measure. For this thing I besought the Lord thrice, that it might depart from me. And he said unto me, My grace is sufficient for thee: for my strength is made perfect in weakness. Most gladly therefore will I rather glory in my infirmities, that the power of Christ may rest upon me.

2 CORINTHIANS 12:7–9 KJV

Weeping may remain for a night, but rejoicing comes in the morning.

PSALM 30:5 NIV

The righteous cry out, and the LORD hears, and delivers them out of all their troubles.

PSALM 34:17 NKJV

"Blessed are you who hunger now, for you shall be satisfied. Blessed are you who weep now, for you shall laugh. Blessed are you when men hate you, and ostracize you, and insult you, and scorn your name as evil, for the sake of the Son of Man. Be glad in that day and leap for joy, for behold, your reward is great in heaven. For in the same way their fathers used to treat the prophets."

LUKE 6:21–23 NASB

"I have told you all this so that you may have peace in me. Here on earth you will have many trials and sorrows. But take heart, because I have overcome the world."

JOHN 16:33 NLT

In this you greatly rejoice, even though now for a little while, if necessary, you have been distressed by various trials, so that the proof of your faith, being more precious than gold which is perishable, even though tested by fire, may be found to result in praise and glory and honor at the revelation of Jesus Christ.

1 PETER 1:6–7 NASB

After you have suffered for a little while,
the God of all grace,
who called you to His eternal glory in Christ,
will Himself perfect, confirm,
strengthen and establish you.

1 PETER 5:10 NASB

Blessed is the man who endures temptation; for when he has been approved, he will receive the crown of life which the Lord has promised to those who love Him.

JAMES 1:12 NKJV

For I consider that the sufferings of this present time are not worthy to be compared with the glory that is to be revealed to us.

ROMANS 8:18 NASB

Rejoicing in hope, persevering in tribulation, devoted to prayer. . .

ROMANS 12:12 NASB

Lord,

it really hurts when I'm knocked down by difficulties in life.
Thank You for always being with me
and helping me over each hurdle.
Please give me strength
and help me to learn the lessons
You want to teach me in the hard times.
Amen.

Anger

Y ou've probably heard the old saying, "Don't get mad, get even." Well, here's some good advice for you: Don't do either. Anger robs people of the joy of the Christian life. On the other hand, being quick to forgive will help you defeat those angry feelings. Ask God for His strength to swap your anger for His joy.

My dear brothers, take note of this: Everyone should be quick to listen, slow to speak and slow to become angry, for man's anger does not bring about the righteous life that God desires.

JAMES 1:19-20 NIV

Do not associate with a man given to anger; or go with a hot-tempered man, or you will learn his ways and find a snare for yourself.

PROVERBS 22:24–25 NASB

F̲or every minute
you are angry,
you lose sixty seconds
of happiness.

RALPH WALDO EMERSON

Don't be quick-tempered, for anger is the friend of fools.

ECCLESIASTES 7:9 NLT

The discretion of a man makes him slow to anger, and his glory is to overlook a transgression.

PROVERBS 19:11 NKJV

A fool's wrath is presently known: but a prudent man covereth shame.

PROVERBS 12:16 KJV

"For wrath kills a foolish man, and envy slays a simple one."

JOB 5:2 NKJV

Do all things without grumbling or disputing.

PHILIPPIANS 2:14 NASB

Be angry, and yet do not sin; do not let the sun go down on your anger, and do not give the devil an opportunity. . . . Let all bitterness and wrath and anger and clamor and slander be put away from you, along with all malice.

EPHESIANS 4:26–27, 31 NASB

"But I say to you that whoever is angry with his brother without a cause shall be in danger of the judgment. And whoever says to his brother, 'Raca!' shall be in danger of the council. But whoever says, 'You fool!' shall be in danger of hell fire."

MATTHEW 5:22 NKJV

A gentle answer turns away wrath, but a harsh word stirs up anger. . . . A hot-tempered man stirs up strife, but the slow to anger calms a dispute.

PROVERBS 15:1, 18 NASB

Dear friends, never avenge yourselves. Leave that to God. For it is written, "I will take vengeance; I will repay those who deserve it," says the Lord.

ROMANS 12:19 NLT

Starting a quarrel is like breaching a dam; so drop the matter before a dispute breaks out.

PROVERBS 17:14 NIV

A man of great wrath will suffer punishment; for if you rescue him, you will have to do it again.

PROVERBS 19:19 NKJV

Cease from anger and forsake wrath; do not fret; it leads only to evildoing.

PSALM 37:8 NASB

He that is soon angry dealeth foolishly. . . . He that is slow to wrath is of great understanding: but he that is hasty of spirit exalteth folly.

PROVERBS 14:17, 29 KJV

But now you yourselves are to put off all these: anger, wrath, malice, blasphemy, filthy language out of your mouth.

COLOSSIANS 3:8 NKJV

Dear God,

please help me to control my anger.
Nothing good comes from doing things out of rage.
I will only hurt You, myself, and others.
I want Your Spirit to control my words and actions.
Fill me with Your peace
so that I can react to unpleasant situations
in a way that's pleasing to You.
Amen.

Conversation

Like a comic book superhero, you possess an amazing power—the words you say. With words, you can affect another person's life dramatically—in either a positive or a negative way. Think hard about the words you say *before* you say them; unlike computer files, those words can't be erased once they've been spoken. Make it a point always to speak positively—words of kindness, helpfulness, and mercy. Use your "power" for good!

When words are many, sin is not absent, but he who holds his tongue is wise.

PROVERBS 10:19 NIV

"A good man out of the good treasure of his heart brings forth good things, and an evil man out of the evil treasure brings forth evil things. But I say to you that for every idle word men may speak, they will give account of it in the day of judgment. For by your words you will be justified, and by your words you will be condemned."

MATTHEW 12:35–37 NKJV

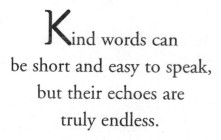

Kind words can
be short and easy to speak,
but their echoes are
truly endless.

MOTHER TERESA

Do not speak evil of one another, brethren. He who speaks evil of a brother and judges his brother, speaks evil of the law and judges the law. But if you judge the law, you are not a doer of the law but a judge.

JAMES 4:11 NKJV

A man has joy in an apt answer, and how delightful is a timely word!

PROVERBS 15:23 NASB

For the Scriptures say, "If you want a happy life and good days, keep your tongue from speaking evil, and keep your lips from telling lies."

1 PETER 3:10 NLT

Let your speech always be with grace, as though seasoned with salt, so that you will know how you should respond to each person.

COLOSSIANS 4:6 NASB

But now ye also put off all these; anger, wrath, malice, blasphemy, filthy communication out of your mouth.

COLOSSIANS 3:8 KJV

If anyone thinks himself to be religious, and yet does not bridle his tongue but deceives his own heart, this man's religion is worthless.

JAMES 1:26 NASB

Let no corrupt word proceed out of your mouth, but what is good for necessary edification, that it may impart grace to the hearers.

EPHESIANS 4:29 NKJV

"When they bring you before the synagogues and the rulers and the authorities, do not worry about how or what you are to speak in your defense, or what you are to say; for the Holy Spirit will teach you in that very hour what you ought to say."

LUKE 12:11–12 NASB

Set a watch, O LORD, before my mouth; keep the door of my lips.

PSALM 141:3 KJV

I said, "I will watch my ways and keep my tongue from sin; I will put a muzzle on my mouth as long as the wicked are in my presence."

PSALM 39:1 NIV

For we all stumble in many ways. If anyone does not stumble in what he says, he is a perfect man, able to bridle the whole body as well. Now if we put the bits into the horses' mouths so that they will obey us, we direct their entire body as well. Look at the ships also, though they are so great and are driven by strong winds, are still directed by a very small rudder wherever the inclination of the pilot desires. So also the tongue is a small part of the body, and yet it boasts of great things. See how great a forest is set aflame by such a small fire! And the tongue is a fire, the very world of iniquity; the tongue is set among our members as that which defiles the entire body, and sets on fire the course of our life, and is set on fire by hell. For every species of beasts and birds, of reptiles and creatures of the sea, is tamed and has been tamed by the human race. But no one can tame the tongue; it is a restless evil and full of deadly poison. With it we bless our Lord and Father, and with it we curse men, who have been made in the likeness of God; from the same mouth come both blessing and cursing. My brethren, these things ought not to be this way.

JAMES 3:2–10 NASB

He who restrains his words has knowledge, and he who has a cool spirit is a man of understanding.

PROVERBS 17:27 NASB

He who guards his mouth and his tongue keeps himself from calamity.

PROVERBS 21:23 NIV

A fool vents all his feelings, but a wise man holds them back.

PROVERBS 29:11 NKJV

Do you see a man hasty in his words? There is more hope for a fool than for him.

PROVERBS 29:20 NKJV

Heavenly Father,

please guard my tongue.
I don't want to hurt others with mean or thoughtless words.
I want to speak only words that will
encourage others and build them up.
Amen.

Counsel

Who you gonna listen to? Modern society, through television, movies, and popular music, will give you plenty of advice—most all of it bad. Taking counsel from God and committed Christians, though, will provide an entirely different perspective—the *right* one. Choose to follow God's counsel—He is perfect and has laid out clear instructions to obey in His Word, the Bible. He'll also use other Christians to help guide you in the decisions that you must make—and you'll have plenty.

The way of a fool is right in his own eyes, but a wise man is he who listens to counsel.

PROVERBS 12:15 NASB

Then Jehoshaphat added, "But first let's find out what the LORD says."

1 KINGS 22:5 NLT

Appreciate
the commands of scripture
as much as the promises.

BRUCE & STAN

Listen to counsel and accept discipline, that you may be wise the rest of your days.

PROVERBS 19:20 NASB

For unto us a Child is born, unto us a Son is given; and the government will be upon His shoulder. And His name will be called Wonderful, Counselor.

ISAIAH 9:6 NKJV

Howbeit when he, the Spirit of truth, is come, he will guide you into all truth: for he shall not speak of himself; but whatsoever he shall hear, that shall he speak: and he will shew you things to come.

JOHN 16:13 KJV

All your children shall be taught by the LORD, and great shall be the peace of your children.

ISAIAH 54:13 NKJV

All discipline for the moment seems not to be joyful, but sorrowful; yet to those who have been trained by it, afterwards it yields the peaceful fruit of righteousness.

HEBREWS 12:11 NASB

Instruct a wise man and he will be wiser still; teach a righteous man and he will add to his learning.

PROVERBS 9:9 NIV

Brethren, if a man is overtaken in any trespass, you who are spiritual restore such a one in a spirit of gentleness, considering yourself lest you also be tempted.

GALATIANS 6:1 NKJV

They should gently teach those who oppose the truth. Perhaps God will change those people's hearts, and they will believe the truth.

2 TIMOTHY 2:25 NLT

"With Him are wisdom and strength, He has counsel and understanding."

PSALM — JOB 12:13 NKJV

Oil and perfume make the heart glad, so a man's counsel is sweet to his friend.

PROVERBS 27:9 NASB

I will instruct thee and teach thee in the way which thou shalt go: I will guide thee with mine eye.

PSALM 32:8 KJV

"And those of the people who understand shall instruct many."

DANIEL 11:33 NKJV

Where there is no guidance the people fall, but in abundance of counselors there is victory.

PROVERBS 11:14 NASB

The Spirit of the LORD will rest on him—the Spirit of wisdom and of understanding, the Spirit of counsel and of power, the Spirit of knowledge and of the fear of the LORD.

ISAIAH 11:2 NIV

Blessed is the man who walks not in the counsel of the ungodly, nor stands in the path of sinners, nor sits in the seat of the scornful.

PSALM 1:1 NKJV

Without consultation, plans are frustrated, but with many counselors they succeed.

PROVERBS 15:22 NASB

The LORD Almighty is a wonderful teacher, and he gives the farmer great wisdom.

ISAIAH 28:29 NLT

You will guide me with Your counsel, and afterward receive me to glory.

PSALM 73:24 NKJV

A wise man will hear and increase in learning, and a man of understanding will acquire wise counsel.

PROVERBS 1:5 NASB

Dear Lord,
what should I do?
I have a big decision to make and need some direction.
Please show me what You'd have me to do,
and help me not be too proud to ask others for their help.
Amen.

Courage

Courage isn't skiing down the vertical face of a mountain, one step ahead of an advancing avalanche. (*Crazy,* maybe.) Courage is doing the right thing, even when "the right thing" scares you. You'll have to make many decisions in life. Resolve today that, with God's help, you will have the courage to make the right choices—every time.

So that we may boldly say, The Lord is my helper, and I will not fear what man shall do unto me.

HEBREWS 13:6 KJV

For God has not given us a spirit of fear, but of power and of love and of a sound mind.

2 TIMOTHY 1:7 NKJV

Courage is contagious.
When a brave man takes a stand,
the spines of others are often stiffened.

BILLY GRAHAM

By this, love is perfected with us, so that we may have confidence in the day of judgment; because as He is, so also are we in this world.

1 JOHN 4:17 NASB

We have boldness and access with confidence through faith in Him.

EPHESIANS 3:12 NKJV

And now, dear children, continue to live in fellowship with Christ so that when he returns, you will be full of courage and not shrink back from him in shame.

1 JOHN 2:28 NLT

Whatever happens, conduct yourselves in a manner worthy of the gospel of Christ. Then, whether I come and see you or only hear about you in my absence, I will know that you stand firm in one spirit, contending as one man for the faith of the gospel without being frightened in any way by those who oppose you. This is a sign to them that they will be destroyed, but that you will be saved—and that by God.

PHILIPPIANS 1:27–28 NIV

In the fear of the LORD there is strong confidence, and His children will have a place of refuge.

PROVERBS 14:26 NKJV

We have confidence to enter the holy place by the blood of Jesus.

HEBREWS 10:19 NASB

For the LORD will be your confidence and will keep your foot from being caught.

PROVERBS 3:26 NASB

And thou, son of man, be not afraid of them, neither be afraid of their words, though briers and thorns be with thee, and thou dost dwell among scorpions: be not afraid of their words, nor be dismayed at their looks, though they be a rebellious house.

EZEKIEL 2:6 KJV

Be brave, be strong.

1 CORINTHIANS 16:13 NKJV

Dear friends, if our hearts do not condemn us, we have confidence before God.

1 JOHN 3:21 NIV

Therefore let us draw near with confidence to the throne of grace, so that we may receive mercy and find grace to help in time of need.

HEBREWS 4:16 NASB

The wicked flee when no one pursues, but the righteous are bold as a lion.

PROVERBS 28:1 NKJV

Be strong and let your heart take courage, all you who hope in the LORD.

PSALM 31:24 NASB

"By standing firm, you will win your souls."

LUKE 21:19 NLT

I can do all things through Christ who strengthens me.

PHILIPPIANS 4:13 NKJV

Lord,

I pray for the courage I need in life.
Make me a strong Christian—
one who knows that You will be right beside me,
helping me to make the right choices.
Amen.

Discipline

"This is going to hurt me more than it hurts you" is an old line fathers used before spanking their children. Kids have joked about it for years, but it's true—punishment is no fun for anyone involved. It's still vital, though.

Like human fathers, God must correct His children when they disobey Him—and it's all because of His profound love. He truly cares enough to discipline us when we stray from Him. Nobody likes to be punished, but when we learn from our errors, we come closer to God.

"Thus you are to know in your heart that the LORD your God was disciplining you just as a man disciplines his son."

DEUTERONOMY 8:5 NASB

God has to punish
His children from time to time,
and it is the very demonstration
of His love.

ELISABETH ELLIOT

But when we are judged, we are chastened of the Lord, that we should not be condemned with the world.

1 CORINTHIANS 11:32 KJV

He who keeps instruction is in the way of life, but he who refuses correction goes astray.

PROVERBS 10:17 NKJV

"Behold, how happy is the man whom God reproves, so do not despise the discipline of the Almighty. For He inflicts pain, and gives relief; He wounds, and His hands also heal."

JOB 5:17–18 NASB

And you have forgotten that word of encouragement that addresses you as sons: "My son, do not make light of the Lord's discipline, and do not lose heart when he rebukes you, because the Lord disciplines those he loves, and he punishes everyone he accepts as a son." Endure hardship as discipline; God is treating you as sons. For what son is not disciplined by his father? If you are not disciplined (and everyone undergoes discipline), then you are illegitimate children and not true sons. Moreover, we have all had human fathers who disciplined us and we respected them for it. How much more should we submit to the Father of our spirits and live! Our fathers disciplined us for a little while as they thought best; but God disciplines us for our good, that we may share in his holiness. No discipline seems pleasant at the time, but painful. Later on, however, it produces a harvest of righteousness and peace for those who have been trained by it.

HEBREWS 12:5–11 NIV

The fear of the LORD is the beginning of knowledge, but fools despise wisdom and instruction.

PROVERBS 1:7 NKJV

He who chastens the nations, will He not rebuke, even He who teaches man knowledge?

PSALM 94:10 NASB

Blessed is the man whom You chasten, O LORD, and whom You teach out of Your law; that You may grant him relief from the days of adversity, until a pit is dug for the wicked.

PSALM 94:12–13 NASB

For these commands and this teaching are a lamp to light the way ahead of you. The correction of discipline is the way to life.

PROVERBS 6:23 NLT

"As many as I love, I rebuke and chasten. Therefore be zealous and repent."

REVELATION 3:19 NKJV

For whom the LORD loveth he correcteth; even as a father the son in whom he delighteth.

PROVERBS 3:12 KJV

Thank You
for loving me enough to discipline me, God.
I'm so sorry for the times that I don't obey You.
Help me to learn from my mistakes
so that I can become more like You.
Amen.

Encouragement

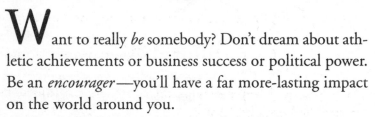

Want to really *be* somebody? Don't dream about athletic achievements or business success or political power. Be an *encourager*—you'll have a far more-lasting impact on the world around you.

Encouragement comes in many forms: a smile, a telephone call, a note, the gift of your time. Make these uplifting acts a habit, and you can change the world—at least your little part of it. Even though you may never know all the effects of your encouragement, be assured that others will remember you as somebody special.

Pure and undefiled religion before God and the Father is this: to visit orphans and widows in their trouble, and to keep oneself unspotted from the world.

JAMES 1:27 NKJV

Now the God of patience and consolation grant you to be likeminded one toward another according to Christ Jesus.

ROMANS 15:5 KJV

If we are distressed, it is for your comfort and salvation; if we are comforted, it is for your comfort, which produces in you patient endurance of the same sufferings we suffer.

2 CORINTHIANS 1:6 NIV

Therefore encourage one another and build up one another, just as you also are doing.

1 THESSALONIANS 5:11 NASB

The light of the eyes rejoices the heart, and a good report makes the bones healthy.

PROVERBS 15:30 NKJV

Don't think only about your own affairs, but be interested in others, too, and what they are doing.

PHILIPPIANS 2:4 NLT

He gives power to the weak, and to those who have no might He increases strength.

ISAIAH 40:29 NKJV

Little children, let us not love with word or with tongue, but in deed and truth.

1 JOHN 3:18 NASB

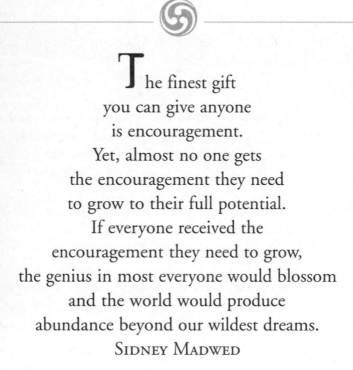

The finest gift
you can give anyone
is encouragement.
Yet, almost no one gets
the encouragement they need
to grow to their full potential.
If everyone received the
encouragement they need to grow,
the genius in most everyone would blossom
and the world would produce
abundance beyond our wildest dreams.

SIDNEY MADWED

Bear one another's burdens, and so fulfill the law of Christ.

GALATIANS 6:2 NKJV

So then, brethren, stand firm and hold to the traditions which you were taught, whether by word of mouth or by letter from us. Now may our Lord Jesus Christ Himself and God our Father, who has loved us and given us eternal comfort and good hope by grace, comfort and strengthen your hearts in every good work and word.

2 THESSALONIANS 2:15–17 NASB

Heavenly Father,

Thank You for those special people who
make my day better by speaking an encouraging word
or doing something kind for me.
I want to be an encouragement to others, too.
Help me to build up those around me
with uplifting words and actions.
Amen.

Eternal Life

You're young, and life seems long. But soon you'll realize that you've been out of school for five, ten, twenty years. . .and you'll know what the Bible means when it says life is "a mist that appears for a little while and then vanishes" (James 4:14 NIV). We can all be thankful that that's not the end of the story—God has promised *eternal* life to those who give their earthly lives to Him. That's a great trade! Live this life in gratitude for God's love to you.

"Do not work for the food which perishes, but for the food which endures to eternal life, which the Son of Man will give to you, for on Him the Father, God, has set His seal."

JOHN 6:27 NASB

"And everyone who has left houses or brothers or sisters or father or mother or children or fields for my sake will receive a hundred times as much and will inherit eternal life."

MATTHEW 19:29 NIV

When you were born,
you cried and everybody else was happy.
The only question that matters is this:
When you die,
will you be happy when everybody else is crying?

TONY CAMPOLO

For the one who sows to his own flesh will from the flesh reap corruption, but the one who sows to the Spirit will from the Spirit reap eternal life.

GALATIANS 6:8 NASB

The Spirit of God, who raised Jesus from the dead, lives in you. And just as he raised Christ from the dead, he will give life to your mortal body by this same Spirit living within you.

ROMANS 8:11 NLT

And when the Chief Shepherd appears, you will receive the crown of glory that does not fade away.

1 PETER 5:4 NKJV

The world is passing away, and also its lusts; but the one who does the will of God lives forever.

1 JOHN 2:17 NASB

"Most assuredly, I say to you, he who believes in Me has everlasting life."

JOHN 6:47 NKJV

"Most assuredly, I say to you, he who hears My word and believes in Him who sent Me has everlasting life, and shall not come into judgment, but has passed from death into life."

JOHN 5:24 NKJV

That being justified by his grace, we should be made heirs according to the hope of eternal life.

TITUS 3:7 KJV

For we know that if our earthly house, this tent, is destroyed, we have a building from God, a house not made with hands, eternal in the heavens.

2 CORINTHIANS 5:1 NKJV

"He who loves his life loses it, and he who hates his life in this world will keep it to life eternal."

JOHN 12:25 NASB

"For this reason, they are before the throne of God; and they serve Him day and night in His temple; and He who sits on the throne will spread His tabernacle over them. They will hunger no longer, nor thirst anymore; nor will the sun beat down on them, nor any heat; for the Lamb in the center of the throne will be their shepherd, and will guide them to springs of the water of life; and God will wipe every tear from their eyes."

REVELATION 7:15–17 NASB

We know also that the Son of God has come and has given us understanding, so that we may know him who is true. And we are in him who is true—even in his Son Jesus Christ. He is the true God and eternal life.

1 JOHN 5:20 NIV

Jesus said to her, "I am the resurrection and the life; he who believes in Me will live even if he dies, and everyone who lives and believes in Me will never die. Do you believe this?"

JOHN 11:25–26 NASB

But now that you have been set free from sin and have become slaves to God, the benefit you reap leads to holiness, and the result is eternal life. For the wages of sin is death, but the gift of God is eternal life in Christ Jesus our Lord.

ROMANS 6:22–23 NIV

Keep yourselves in God's love as you wait for the mercy of our Lord Jesus Christ to bring you to eternal life.

JUDE 21 NIV

Blessed be the God and Father of our Lord Jesus Christ, who according to His great mercy has caused us to be born again to a living hope through the resurrection of Jesus Christ from the dead, to obtain an inheritance which is imperishable and undefiled and will not fade away, reserved in heaven for you, who are protected by the power of God through faith for a salvation ready to be revealed in the last time.

1 PETER 1:3–5 NASB

He will give eternal life to those who
persist in doing what is good,
seeking after the glory and honor
and immortality that God offers.

ROMANS 2:7 NLT

This truth gives them the confidence of eternal life, which God promised them before the world began—and he cannot lie.

TITUS 1:2 NLT

For God so loved the world, that he gave his only begotten Son, that whosoever believeth in him should not perish, but have everlasting life.

JOHN 3:16 KJV

And this is the testimony: that God has given us eternal life, and this life is in His Son. He who has the Son has life; he who does not have the Son of God does not have life. These things I have written to you who believe in the name of the Son of God, that you may know that you have eternal life, and that you may continue to believe in the name of the Son of God.

1 JOHN 5:11–13 NKJV

And this is eternal life,
that they may know You, the only true God,
and Jesus Christ whom You have sent."

JOHN 17:3 NKJV

Let that therefore abide in you, which ye have heard from the beginning. If that which ye have heard from the beginning shall remain in you, ye also shall continue in the Son, and in the Father. And this is the promise that he hath promised us, even eternal life.

1 JOHN 2:24–25 KJV

There shall be no night there: They need no lamp nor light of the sun, for the Lord God gives them light. And they shall reign forever and ever.

REVELATION 22:5 NKJV

Behold, I tell you a mystery: We shall not all sleep, but we shall all be changed—in a moment, in the twinkling of an eye, at the last trumpet. For the trumpet will sound, and the dead will be raised incorruptible, and we shall be changed. For this corruptible must put on incorruption, and this mortal must put on immortality. So when this corruptible has put on incorruption, and this mortal has put on immortality, then shall be brought to pass the saying that is written: "Death is swallowed up in victory."

1 CORINTHIANS 15:51–54 NKJV

"Many of those who sleep in the dust of the ground will awake, these to everlasting life, but the others to disgrace and everlasting contempt."

DANIEL 12:2 NASB

Fight the good fight of faith; take hold of the eternal life to which you were called, and you made the good confession in the presence of many witnesses.

1 TIMOTHY 6:12 NASB

"In my Father's house are many rooms; if it were not so, I would have told you. I am going there to prepare a place for you. And if I go and prepare a place for you, I will come back and take you to be with me that you also may be where I am."

JOHN 14:2–3 NIV

"And I give them eternal life, and they shall never perish; neither shall anyone snatch them out of My hand."

JOHN 10:28 NKJV

In the future there is laid up for me the crown of righteousness, which the Lord, the righteous Judge, will award to me on that day; and not only to me, but also to all who have loved His appearing.

2 TIMOTHY 4:8 NASB

Lord,
*I don't know how long I have to live,
but I do know that You are preparing a
wonderful place for me when this life is over.
Thank You for giving me the gift of
eternal life in heaven with You.
Amen.*

Faith

Y a gotta have faith," many say. The question is, faith in what? Make sure you put your faith in something (actually, *Someone*) worthy. In a word, *God*.

Of course, in a world of uncertainty, faith sometimes seems out of reach. But remember this: God exists, and He never changes. We can put our complete faith in Him, and He will never fail us.

For we walk by faith, not by sight.

2 CORINTHIANS 5:7 NKJV

In addition to all, taking up the shield of faith with which you will be able to extinguish all the flaming arrows of the evil one.

EPHESIANS 6:16 NASB

Faith means
believing that Jesus is
who He says He is (God),
that He did what He said He did
(died for our sins),
and that He will do for us
what He said He would do
(forgive our sins and give us eternal life).

PATRICK MORLEY

Now the purpose of the commandment is love from a pure heart, from a good conscience, and from sincere faith.

1 TIMOTHY 1:5 NKJV

Listen, my dear brothers: Has not God chosen those who are poor in the eyes of the world to be rich in faith and to inherit the kingdom he promised those who love him?

JAMES 2:5 NIV

Trust in the LORD with all your heart, and lean not on your own understanding.

PROVERBS 3:5 NKJV

"For I will certainly rescue you, and you will not fall by the sword; but you will have your own life as booty, because you have trusted in Me," declares the LORD.

JEREMIAH 39:18 NASB

For when your faith is tested, your endurance has a chance to grow. So let it grow, for when your endurance is fully developed, you will be strong in character and ready for anything.

JAMES 1:3–4 NLT

And He said to the woman, "Your faith has saved you; go in peace."

LUKE 7:50 NASB

Now faith is the substance of things hoped for, the evidence of things not seen.

HEBREWS 11:1 KJV

This charge I commit to you, son Timothy, according to the prophecies previously made concerning you, that by them you may wage the good warfare, having faith and a good conscience.

1 TIMOTHY 1:18–19 NKJV

But as many as received Him, to them He gave the right to become children of God, even to those who believe in His name.

JOHN 1:12 NASB

And my speech and my preaching were not with persuasive words of human wisdom, but in demonstration of the Spirit and of power, that your faith should not be in the wisdom of men but in the power of God.

1 CORINTHIANS 2:4–5 NKJV

"Have faith in God," Jesus answered. "I tell you the truth, if anyone says to this mountain, 'Go, throw yourself into the sea,' and does not doubt in his heart but believes that what he says will happen, it will be done for him. Therefore I tell you, whatever you ask for in prayer, believe that you have received it, and it will be yours."

MARK 11:22–24 NIV

That He would grant you, according to the riches of His glory, to be strengthened with might through His Spirit in the inner man, that Christ may dwell in your hearts through faith; that you, being rooted and grounded in love, may be able to comprehend with all the saints what is the width and length and depth and height—to know the love of Christ which passes knowledge; that you may be filled with all the fullness of God.

EPHESIANS 3:16–19 NKJV

Thou wilt keep him in perfect peace, whose mind is stayed on thee: because he trusteth in thee.

ISAIAH 26:3 KJV

I myself no longer live, but Christ lives in me. So I live my life in this earthly body by trusting in the Son of God, who loved me and gave himself for me.

GALATIANS 2:20 NLT

F or in it the righteousness of God
is revealed from faith to faith;
as it is written,
"But the righteous man shall live by faith."

ROMANS 1:17 NASB

So the Lord said, "If you have faith as a mustard seed, you can say to this mulberry tree, 'Be pulled up by the roots and be planted in the sea,' and it would obey you."

LUKE 17:6 NKJV

"Blessed is the man who trusts in the LORD and whose trust is the LORD. For he will be like a tree planted by the water, that extends its roots by a stream and will not fear when the heat comes; but its leaves will be green, and it will not be anxious in a year of drought nor cease to yield fruit."

JEREMIAH 17:7–8 NASB

Watch, stand fast in the faith.

1 CORINTHIANS 16:13 NKJV

Let us go right into the presence of God, with true hearts fully trusting him. For our evil consciences have been sprinkled with Christ's blood to make us clean, and our bodies have been washed with pure water.

HEBREWS 10:22 NLT

And though you have not seen Him, you love Him, and though you do not see Him now, but believe in Him, you greatly rejoice with joy inexpressible and full of glory.

1 PETER 1:8 NASB

Is any one of you sick? He should call the elders of the church to pray over him and anoint him with oil in the name of the Lord. And the prayer offered in faith will make the sick person well; the Lord will raise him up. If he has sinned, he will be forgiven.

JAMES 5:14–15 NIV

For you are all sons of God through faith in Christ Jesus.

GALATIANS 3:26 NKJV

Jesus saith unto him, Thomas, because thou hast seen me, thou hast believed: blessed are they that have not seen, and yet have believed.

JOHN 20:29 KJV

So then faith comes by hearing, and hearing by the word of God.

ROMANS 10:17 NKJV

But if any of you lacks wisdom, let him ask of God, who gives to all generously and without reproach, and it will be given to him. But he must ask in faith without any doubting, for the one who doubts is like the surf of the sea, driven and tossed by the wind.

JAMES 1:5–6 NASB

And without faith it is impossible to please Him, for he who comes to God must believe that He is and that He is a rewarder of those who seek Him.

HEBREWS 11:6 NASB

"Everything is possible for him who believes."

MARK 9:23 NIV

Dear God,

help me to grow in faith.
Continue to teach me that
I don't have to know what the future holds—
You're already there.
Help me to turn over complete control of my life to You,
because You will always take care of me
and will never let me down.
Amen.

Finances

Surveys often show that "making money" is a top priority of graduating college seniors. Sure, we all need money to live on. . .but should a fat bank account be our primary goal?

Money is a source of both joy and trial in our lives. In the proper perspective, money can be a useful, helpful thing. The wrong emphasis, however, can lead to grief—and possibly sin. God has a lot to say about money in the Bible—learn His priorities, and honor Him with your finances.

A good name is to be chosen rather than great riches, loving favor rather than silver and gold. . . . By humility and the fear of the LORD are riches and honor and life.

PROVERBS 22:1, 4 NKJV

Make sure that your character is free from the love of money, being content with what you have; for He Himself has said, "I will never desert you, nor will I ever forsake you."

HEBREWS 13:5 NASB

Do not withhold good from those who deserve it when it's in your power to help them. If you can help your neighbor now, don't say, "Come back tomorrow, and then I'll help you."

PROVERBS 3:27–28 NLT

"Give, and it will be given to you: good measure, pressed down, shaken together, and running over will be put into your bosom. For with the same measure that you use, it will be measured back to you."

LUKE 6:38 NKJV

But those who want to get rich fall into temptation and a snare and many foolish and harmful desires which plunge men into ruin and destruction. For the love of money is a root of all sorts of evil, and some by longing for it have wandered away from the faith and pierced themselves with many griefs. But flee from these things, you man of God, and pursue righteousness, godliness, faith, love, perseverance and gentleness.

1 TIMOTHY 6:9–11 NASB

The rich ruleth over the poor, and the borrower is servant
to the lender.

PROVERBS 22:7 KJV

W e should] spend
no more than we make
on a monthly basis.
Ideally that means to
live on a cash basis and
not use credit or borrowed money
to provide normal living expenses.
It also means the
self-discipline to control spending
and keep needs, wants, and desires
in their proper relationship.

LARRY BURKETT

In this case, moreover, it is required of stewards that one be
found trustworthy.

1 CORINTHIANS 4:2 NASB

Do not be among those who give pledges, among those who become guarantors for debts. If you have nothing with which to pay, why should he take your bed from under you?

PROVERBS 22:26–27 NASB

And He said to them, "Render therefore to Caesar the things that are Caesar's, and to God the things that are God's."

MATTHEW 22:21 NKJV

LORD, who shall abide in thy tabernacle? who shall dwell in thy holy hill? . . . He that putteth not out his money to usury, nor taketh reward against the innocent. He that doeth these things shall never be moved.

PSALM 15:1, 5 KJV

"Every man shall give as he is able, according to the blessing of the LORD your God which He has given you."

DEUTERONOMY 16:17 NASB

Riches do not profit in the day of wrath, but righteousness delivers from death.

PROVERBS 11:4 NKJV

"For which of you, intending to build a tower, does not sit down first and count the cost, whether he has enough to finish it—lest, after he has laid the foundation, and is not able to finish, all who see it begin to mock him, saying, 'This man began to build and was not able to finish.' "

LUKE 14:28–30 NKJV

"I tell you, use worldly wealth to gain friends for yourselves, so that when it is gone, you will be welcomed into eternal dwellings. Whoever can be trusted with very little can also be trusted with much, and whoever is dishonest with very little will also be dishonest with much. So if you have not been trustworthy in handling worldly wealth, who will trust you with true riches? And if you have not been trustworthy with someone else's property, who will give you property of your own?"

LUKE 16:9–12 NIV

He who trusts in his riches will fall,
but the righteous will flourish
like the green leaf.

PROVERBS 11:28 NASB

And it is a good thing to receive wealth from God and the good health to enjoy it. To enjoy your work and accept your lot in life—that is indeed a gift from God.

ECCLESIASTES 5:19 NLT

Some who are poor pretend to be rich; others who are rich pretend to be poor.

PROVERBS 13:7 NLT

"No one can serve two masters; for either he will hate the one and love the other, or else he will be loyal to the one and despise the other. You cannot serve God and mammon."

MATTHEW 6:24 NKJV

"I have shown you in every way, by laboring like this, that you must support the weak. And remember the words of the Lord Jesus, that He said, 'It is more blessed to give than to receive.'"

ACTS 20:35 NKJV

"But you shall remember the LORD your God, for it is He who is giving you power to make wealth, that He may confirm His covenant which He swore to your fathers, as it is this day."

DEUTERONOMY 8:18 NASB

"So when you give to the needy, do not announce it with trumpets, as the hypocrites do in the synagogues and on the streets, to be honored by men. I tell you the truth, they have received their reward in full. But when you give to the needy, do not let your left hand know what your right hand is doing, so that your giving may be in secret. Then your Father, who sees what is done in secret, will reward you."

MATTHEW 6:2–4 NIV

There is a grievous evil which I have seen under the sun: riches being hoarded by their owner to his hurt. When those riches were lost through a bad investment and he had fathered a son, then there was nothing to support him. As he had come naked from his mother's womb, so will he return as he came. He will take nothing from the fruit of his labor that he can carry in his hand.

ECCLESIASTES 5:13–15 NASB

Command those who are rich in
this present age not to be haughty,
nor to trust in uncertain riches
but in the living God,
who gives us richly all things to enjoy.

1 TIMOTHY 6:17 NKJV

Honour the LORD with thy substance, and with the first-fruits of all thine increase: So shall thy barns be filled with plenty, and thy presses shall burst out with new wine.

PROVERBS 3:9–10 KJV

And He said to them, "Take heed and beware of covetousness, for one's life does not consist in the abundance of the things he possesses."

LUKE 12:15 NKJV

One who is gracious to a poor man lends to the LORD, and He will repay him for his good deed.

PROVERBS 19:17 NASB

Each man should give what he has decided in his heart to give, not reluctantly or under compulsion, for God loves a cheerful giver.

2 CORINTHIANS 9:7 NIV

Let the lowly brother glory in his exaltation, but the rich in his humiliation, because as a flower of the field he will pass away. For no sooner has the sun risen with a burning heat than it withers the grass; its flower falls, and its beautiful appearance perishes. So the rich man also will fade away in his pursuits.

JAMES 1:9–11 NKJV

"And others are the ones on whom seed was sown among the thorns; these are the ones who have heard the word, but the worries of the world, and the deceitfulness of riches, and the desires for other things enter in and choke the word, and it becomes unfruitful."

MARK 4:18–19 NASB

After all, we didn't bring anything with us when we came into the world, and we certainly cannot carry anything with us when we die. So if we have enough food and clothing, let us be content.

1 TIMOTHY 6:7–8 NLT

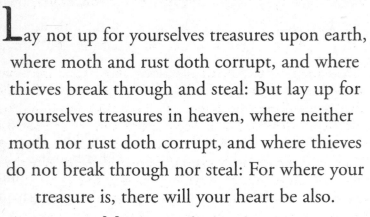

Lay not up for yourselves treasures upon earth, where moth and rust doth corrupt, and where thieves break through and steal: But lay up for yourselves treasures in heaven, where neither moth nor rust doth corrupt, and where thieves do not break through nor steal: For where your treasure is, there will your heart be also.

MATTHEW 6:19–21 KJV

If then you were raised with Christ, seek those things which are above, where Christ is, sitting at the right hand of God. Set your mind on things above, not on things on the earth.

COLOSSIANS 3:1–2 NKJV

Do not trust in oppression and do not vainly hope in robbery; if riches increase, do not set your heart upon them.

PSALM 62:10 NASB

"Give freely without begrudging it, and the LORD your God will bless you in everything you do."

DEUTERONOMY 15:10 NLT

Wealth obtained by fraud dwindles, but the one who gathers by labor increases it.

PROVERBS 13:11 NASB

"Therefore I say to you, do not worry about your life, what you will eat or what you will drink; nor about your body, what you will put on. Is not life more than food and the body more than clothing? Look at the birds of the air, for they neither sow nor reap nor gather into barns; yet your heavenly Father feeds them. Are you not of more value than they? Which of you by worrying can add one cubit to his stature? So why do you worry about clothing? Consider the lilies of the field, how they grow: they neither toil nor spin; and yet I say to you that even Solomon in all his glory was not arrayed like one of these. Now if God so clothes the grass of the field, which today is, and tomorrow is thrown into the oven, will He not much more clothe you, O you of little faith? Therefore do not worry, saying, 'What shall we eat?' or 'What shall we drink?' or 'What shall we wear?' For after all these things the Gentiles seek. For your heavenly Father knows that you need all these things. But seek first the kingdom of God and His righteousness, and all these things shall be added to you."

MATTHEW 6:25–33 NKJV

Heavenly Father,

please help me to keep my financial priorities straight.
I need Your help in controlling my money
and not letting it control me.
Please give me wisdom in the way
I spend the money You've given to me.
Amen.

Forgiveness

How many times have you heard someone say, "I could never forgive him for (list offense here)"? Forgiving others is not easy to do, especially if the other person hasn't asked for forgiveness. But God's Word is clear: We are to forgive others just as He has forgiven us. Wow—too hard, you say? Sure it is, humanly speaking. But God also gives us the ability through His Spirit. Be sure to confess your sins to Him and ask Him to forgive you. Then ask forgiveness of those whom *you* may have offended. Being faithful in these areas will make it easier for you to forgive others.

"No more shall every man teach his neighbor, and every man his brother, saying, 'Know the LORD,' for they all shall know Me, from the least of them to the greatest of them, says the LORD. For I will forgive their iniquity, and their sin I will remember no more."

JEREMIAH 31:34 NKJV

F orgiveness is the oil of relationships.

JOSH MCDOWELL

The discretion of a man makes him slow to anger, and his glory is to overlook a transgression.

PROVERBS 19:11 NKJV

"But I say to you, do not resist an evil person; but whoever slaps you on your right cheek, turn the other to him also. If anyone wants to sue you and take your shirt, let him have your coat also. Whoever forces you to go one mile, go with him two."

MATTHEW 5:39–41 NASB

"And forgive us our sins, for we also forgive everyone who is indebted to us."

LUKE 11:4 NKJV

"Do not judge, and you will not be judged. Do not condemn, and you will not be condemned. Forgive, and you will be forgiven."

LUKE 6:37 NIV

Who is a God like You, pardoning iniquity and passing over the transgression of the remnant of His heritage? He does not retain His anger forever, because He delights in mercy.

MICAH 7:18 NKJV

If we confess our sins, He is faithful and righteous to forgive us our sins and to cleanse us from all unrighteousness.

1 JOHN 1:9 NASB

Bless the LORD, O my soul, and forget none of His benefits; who pardons all your iniquities, who heals all your diseases.

PSALM 103:2–3 NASB

And be ye kind one to another, tenderhearted, forgiving one another, even as God for Christ's sake hath forgiven you.

EPHESIANS 4:32 KJV

"None of their past sins will be brought up again, for they have done what is just and right, and they will surely live."

EZEKIEL 33:16 NLT

Be gracious to me, O God, according to Your lovingkindness; according to the greatness of Your compassion blot out my transgressions.

PSALM 51:1 NASB

"But when you are praying, first forgive anyone you are holding a grudge against, so that your Father in heaven will forgive your sins, too."

MARK 11:25 NLT

"For this is My blood of the new covenant, which is shed for many for the remission of sins."

MATTHEW 26:28 NKJV

Not returning evil for evil or insult for insult, but giving a blessing instead; for you were called for the very purpose that you might inherit a blessing.

1 PETER 3:9 NASB

Take heed to yourselves: If thy brother trespass against thee, rebuke him; and if he repent, forgive him. And if he trespass against thee seven times in a day, and seven times in a day turn again to thee, saying, I repent; thou shalt forgive him.

LUKE 17:3–4 KJV

How blessed is he whose transgression is forgiven, whose sin is covered!

PSALM 32:1 NASB

Therefore, as the elect of God, holy and beloved, put on tender mercies, kindness, humility, meekness, longsuffering; bearing with one another, and forgiving one another, if anyone has a complaint against another; even as Christ forgave you, so you also must do.

COLOSSIANS 3:12–13 NKJV

"For I will forgive their wickedness and will remember their sins no more."

HEBREWS 8:12 NIV

Then Peter came to Jesus and asked, "Lord, how many times shall I forgive my brother when he sins against me? Up to seven times?" Jesus answered, "I tell you, not seven times, but seventy-seven times."

MATTHEW 18:21–22 NIV

"For if you forgive men their trespasses, your heavenly Father will also forgive you. But if you do not forgive men their trespasses, neither will your Father forgive your trespasses."

MATTHEW 6:14–15 NKJV

Lord,

sometimes it's so hard to forgive others,
especially when they have hurt me so badly.
But I know I hurt You when I make the wrong choices,
and yet You forgive me.
Please help me to be like You
and forgive those who wrong me.
Amen.

God's Love

Everybody talks about love. But most of the "love" they're discussing falls far short of the real thing: God's love for His children. God loves with a love beyond human comprehension. He knows everything about you—your needs, your desires, and your dreams—and wants the best for you. That's why He sent His only Son, Jesus, to die on a cross for your sins. Through good times and bad, God will always be with you, loving you more than you could ever imagine.

For it is You who blesses the righteous man, O LORD, You surround him with favor as with a shield.

PSALM 5:12 NASB

"For God so loved the world that he gave his only Son, so that everyone who believes in him will not perish but have eternal life."

JOHN 3:16 NLT

In God, we have a Father
who thinks of us unceasingly.
We are never absent from His thoughts. . . .
And this is a Father who
not only desires to see good in my life,
He has the will and power and wisdom
to cause it to happen!

JAMES ROBISON

And we know that God causes all things to work together for good to those who love God, to those who are called according to His purpose.

ROMANS 8:28 NASB

"Are not five sparrows sold for two copper coins? And not one of them is forgotten before God. But the very hairs of your head are all numbered. Do not fear therefore; you are of more value than many sparrows."

LUKE 12:6–7 NKJV

Those who know your name trust in you, for you, O LORD, have never abandoned anyone who searches for you.

PSALM 9:10 NLT

"Lo, I am with you always, even to the end of the age."

MATTHEW 28:20 NASB

"I will heal their backsliding, I will love them freely, for My anger has turned away from him."

HOSEA 14:4 NKJV

"I knew that you are a gracious and compassionate God, slow to anger and abounding in love, a God who relents from sending calamity."

JONAH 4:2 NIV

"For the LORD your God is a compassionate God; He will not fail you nor destroy you nor forget the covenant with your fathers which He swore to them."

DEUTERONOMY 4:31 NASB

He will fulfil the desire of them that fear him: he also will hear their cry, and will save them. The LORD preserveth all them that love him: but all the wicked will he destroy.

PSALM 145:19–20 KJV

Now hope does not disappoint, because the love of God has been poured out in our hearts by the Holy Spirit who was given to us.

ROMANS 5:5 NKJV

And we have known and believed the love that God has for us. God is love, and he who abides in love abides in God, and God in him.

1 JOHN 4:16 NKJV

For I am persuaded that neither death nor life, nor angels nor principalities nor powers, nor things present nor things to come, nor height nor depth, nor any other created thing, shall be able to separate us from the love of God which is in Christ Jesus our Lord.

ROMANS 8:38–39 NKJV

As for God, His way is blameless; the word of the LORD is tried; He is a shield to all who take refuge in Him.

PSALM 18:30 NASB

God showed how much he loved us by sending his only Son into the world so that we might have eternal life through him. This is real love. It is not that we loved God, but that he loved us and sent his Son as a sacrifice to take away our sins.

1 JOHN 4:9–10 NLT

For the Father himself loveth you, because ye have loved me, and have believed that I came out from God.

JOHN 16:27 KJV

But the LORD is with me as a mighty, awesome One. Therefore my persecutors will stumble, and will not prevail. They will be greatly ashamed, for they will not prosper. Their everlasting confusion will never be forgotten.

JEREMIAH 20:11 NKJV

Every good gift and every perfect gift is from above, and comes down from the Father of lights, with whom there is no variation or shadow of turning. Of His own will He brought us forth by the word of truth, that we might be a kind of firstfruits of His creatures.

JAMES 1:17–18 NKJV

But You, O Lord,
are a God merciful and gracious,
slow to anger and abundant in
lovingkindness and truth.

PSALM 86:15 NASB

The LORD will guard your going out and your coming in from this time forth and forever.

PSALM 121:8 NASB

And my God will meet all your needs according to his glorious riches in Christ Jesus.

PHILIPPIANS 4:19 NIV

Many are the sorrows of the wicked, but he who trusts in the LORD, lovingkindness shall surround him.

PSALM 32:10 NASB

But God showed his great love for us by sending Christ to die for us while we were still sinners.

ROMANS 5:8 NLT

Behold what manner of love the Father has bestowed on us, that we should be called children of God!

1 JOHN 3:1 NKJV

Lord,

I can't imagine the extent of Your love for me.
You sent Your only Son to die for me,
to give me the free gift of eternal life.
I can't think of any greater sacrifice.
Thank You for Your love for me
and that there's nothing I can do
to make You stop loving me.
Amen.

God's Provision

B ut, Mom, I really *need* that new sweater. . . ."

"But, Dad, I really *need* that sports car. . . ."

One of the most important lessons in life is learning to distinguish between *needs* and *wants*. For Christians, the needs are taken care of: God has promised to meet all of them. The wants, of course, are another matter, but as we grow closer to God, they'll likely become less and less of an issue. He knows what is best for us—just trust that He'll take care of you as He has promised.

"For this reason I say to you, do not be worried about your life, as to what you will eat or what you will drink; nor for your body, as to what you will put on. Is not life more than food, and the body more than clothing? Look at the birds of the air, that they do not sow, nor reap nor gather into barns, and yet your heavenly Father feeds them. Are you not worth much more than they? And who of you by being worried can add a single hour to his life? And why are you worried about clothing? Observe how the lilies of the field grow; they do not toil nor do they spin, yet I say to you that not even Solomon in all his glory clothed himself like one of these. But if God so clothes the grass of the field, which is alive today and tomorrow is thrown into the furnace, will He not much more clothe you? You of little faith! Do not worry then, saying, 'What will we eat?' or "What will we drink?' or 'What will we wear for clothing?' For the Gentiles eagerly seek all these things; for your heavenly Father knows that you need all these things. But seek first His kingdom and His righteousness, and all these things will be added to you."

MATTHEW 6:25–33 NASB

Command those who are rich in this present world not to be arrogant nor to put their hope in wealth, which is so uncertain, but to put their hope in God, who richly provides us with everything for our enjoyment.

1 TIMOTHY 6:17 NIV

But my God shall supply all your need according to his riches in glory by Christ Jesus.

PHILIPPIANS 4:19 KJV

The young lions do lack and suffer hunger; but they who seek the LORD shall not be in want of any good thing.

PSALM 34:10 NASB

Lift up your eyes.
Your heavenly Father waits to
bless you in inconceivable ways
to make your life what you
never dreamed it could be.

ANNE ORTLUND

He has given food to those who fear Him; He will ever be mindful of His covenant.

PSALM 111:5 NKJV

Thank You

for providing for my needs—and even my many wants.
The way You take care of me shows me
how valuable I am to You.
I never want to take You or Your wonderful
gifts for granted.
Amen.

Gratitude

Thanksgiving—a day in November, right? Well, not entirely. Thanksgiving should be a continuous attitude expressed by the Christian. We all have many reasons to thank God—take a few minutes to list His blessings, and you'll be amazed at what He's done for you. Give God praise for what He has done in your life—and for what He will do in the future.

I will praise the name of God with a song, and will magnify Him with thanksgiving. This also shall please the LORD better than an ox or bull, which has horns and hooves.

PSALM 69:30–31 NKJV

True thanksgiving means
that we need to thank God
for what He has done for us,
and not to tell Him what
we have done for Him.

GEORGE HENDRICK

Then you will sing psalms and hymns and spiritual songs among yourselves, making music to the Lord in your hearts. And you will always give thanks for everything to God the Father in the name of our Lord Jesus Christ.

EPHESIANS 5:19–20 NLT

Is anyone among you suffering? Then he must pray. Is anyone cheerful? He is to sing praises.

JAMES 5:13 NASB

Oh come, let us sing to the LORD! Let us shout joyfully to the Rock of our salvation. Let us come before His presence with thanksgiving; let us shout joyfully to Him with psalms.

PSALM 95:1–2 NKJV

In everything give thanks; for this is God's will for you in Christ Jesus.

1 THESSALONIANS 5:18 NASB

But thanks be to God, which giveth us the victory through our Lord Jesus Christ.

1 CORINTHIANS 15:57 KJV

I will wash my hands in innocence; so I will go about Your altar, O LORD, that I may proclaim with the voice of thanksgiving, and tell of all Your wondrous works.

PSALM 26:6–7 NKJV

O give thanks to the LORD, for He is good; for His loving-kindness is everlasting.

1 CHRONICLES 16:34 NASB

For every creature of God is good, and nothing to be refused, if it be received with thanksgiving.

1 TIMOTHY 4:4 KJV

He took the seven loaves and the fish; and giving thanks, He broke them and started giving them to the disciples, and the disciples gave them to the people.

MATTHEW 15:36 NASB

And whatever you do or say, let it be as a representative of the Lord Jesus, all the while giving thanks through him to God the Father.

COLOSSIANS 3:17 NLT

I will praise You, O LORD, with my whole heart; I will tell of all Your marvelous works.

PSALM 9:1 NKJV

It is good to give thanks to the LORD, and to sing praises to Your name, O Most High; to declare Your lovingkindness in the morning, and Your faithfulness every night.

PSALM 92:1–2 NKJV

And in that day you will say, "Give thanks to the LORD, call on His name. Make known His deeds among the peoples; make them remember that His name is exalted."

ISAIAH 12:4 NASB

Therefore, since we are receiving a kingdom that cannot be shaken, let us be thankful, and so worship God acceptably with reverence and awe.

HEBREWS 12:28 NIV

Oh, give thanks to the LORD, for He is good! For His mercy endures forever.

PSALM 136:1 NKJV

Lord,

*I'm sorry for the times that I take the things
You've given to me for granted.
Please help me to be thankful
and to express my thanks to others,
but most importantly to You.
Amen.*

Honesty

Let's be honest—honesty is by no means a popular choice in our world today, nor is it an easy one. Look around and you'll see examples of dishonesty every day, from politicians, lawyers, bosses. . .and maybe even ourselves—if we're honest about it! But God expects more of His children. We are commanded to be truthful, as followers of Jesus Christ, who *is* the Truth. Push yourself to be honest, just like you'd push yourself toward any worthwhile goal, and God will bless you for following the truth.

Lying lips are an abomination to the LORD, but those who deal faithfully are His delight.

PROVERBS 12:22 NASB

"I will maintain my righteousness and never let go of it; my conscience will not reproach me as long as I live."

JOB 27:6 NIV

Honesty is the best policy,
as the saying goes.
It works in business as it does in all of life.
Without honesty, relationships fail,
business turns sour,
and self-respect goes right out the door.
Honesty is the bedrock
upon which we build our marriages,
conduct our businesses, and sell our products.
EDWARD HAYES

Honest weights and scales are the LORD's; all the weights in the bag are His work.

PROVERBS 16:11 NKJV

But we have renounced the hidden things of shame, not walking in craftiness nor handling the word of God deceitfully, but by manifestation of the truth commending ourselves to every man's conscience in the sight of God.

2 CORINTHIANS 4:2 NKJV

Pray for us, for we are sure that we have a good conscience, desiring to conduct ourselves honorably in all things.

HEBREWS 13:18 NASB

The LORD abhors dishonest scales, but accurate weights are his delight.

PROVERBS 11:1 NIV

"Do not use dishonest standards when measuring length, weight, or volume. Your scales and weights must be accurate. Your containers for measuring dry goods or liquids must be accurate. I, the LORD, am your God."

LEVITICUS 19:35–36 NLT

"In everything, therefore, treat people the same way you want them to treat you, for this is the Law and the Prophets."

MATTHEW 7:12 NASB

"Do not cheat one another. Do not lie."

LEVITICUS 19:11 NLT

Providing honorable things, not only in the sight of the Lord, but also in the sight of men.

2 CORINTHIANS 8:21 NKJV

And herein do I exercise myself, to have always a conscience void of offence toward God, and toward men.

ACTS 24:16 KJV

Finally, brethren, whatever is true, whatever is honorable, whatever is right, whatever is pure, whatever is lovely, whatever is of good repute, if there is any excellence and if anything worthy of praise, dwell on these things. The things you have learned and received and heard and seen in me, practice these things, and the God of peace will be with you.

PHILIPPIANS 4:8–9 NASB

Who may ascend into the hill of the LORD? And who may stand in His holy place? He who has clean hands and a pure heart, who has not lifted up his soul to falsehood and has not sworn deceitfully.

PSALM 24:3–4 NASB

Do not lie to one another, since you have put off the old man with his deeds, and have put on the new man who is renewed in knowledge according to the image of Him who created him.

COLOSSIANS 3:9–10 NKJV

Dear God,

I want to be known as an honest person.
Cheating is the lazy way out;
please give me the strength and energy
I need to work for my own results.
I want to be the one who says what is true
and lives a life of honesty.
Amen.

Humility

Anyone want to be humiliated? I don't see any hands going up.

While humiliation is a negative thing, humility is very positive—something to be desired. Being humble is not a sign of weakness; you could view it as "quiet strength." Think about Jesus—Philippians 2:8 speaks of Christ's humility, followed by His obedience. He died on the cross for us because of His *humility*. Imagine what great things *you* could accomplish for God if you followed Jesus' humble example.

But he giveth more grace. Wherefore he saith, God resisteth the proud, but giveth grace unto the humble. Submit yourselves therefore to God. Resist the devil, and he will flee from you.

JAMES 4:6–7 KJV

By humility and the fear of the LORD are riches and honor and life.

PROVERBS 22:4 NKJV

D o you aspire to great things?
Begin with little ones.
You desire to erect a very high building?
Think first of the foundation of humility.
The higher you intend it,
the deeper must the foundations be laid.

ST. AUGUSTINE

The humble have seen it and are glad; you who seek God, let your heart revive.

PSALM 69:32 NASB

When pride cometh, then cometh shame: but with the lowly is wisdom.

PROVERBS 11:2 KJV

Your attitude should be the same as that of Christ Jesus: Who, being in very nature God, did not consider equality with God something to be grasped, but made himself nothing, taking the very nature of a servant, being made in human likeness. And being found in appearance as a man, he humbled himself and became obedient to death—even death on a cross! Therefore God exalted him to the highest place and gave him the name that is above every name, that at the name of Jesus every knee should bow, in heaven and on earth and under the earth, and every tongue confess that Jesus Christ is Lord, to the glory of God the Father.

PHILIPPIANS 2:5–11 NIV

"I tell you, this sinner, not the Pharisee, returned home justified before God. For the proud will be humbled, but the humble will be honored."

LUKE 18:14 NLT

For thus says the High and Lofty One who inhabits eternity, whose name is Holy: "I dwell in the high and holy place, with him who has a contrite and humble spirit, to revive the spirit of the humble, and to revive the heart of the contrite ones."

ISAIAH 57:15 NKJV

The fear of the LORD is the instruction for wisdom, and before honor comes humility.

PROVERBS 15:33 NASB

And whosoever shall exalt himself shall be abased; and he that shall humble himself shall be exalted.

MATTHEW 23:12 KJV

You younger men, likewise, be subject to your elders; and all of you, clothe yourselves with humility toward one another, for God is opposed to the proud, but gives grace to the humble. Therefore humble yourselves under the mighty hand of . God, that He may exalt you at the proper time.

1 PETER 5:5–6 NASB

Therefore if there is any consolation in Christ, if any comfort of love, if any fellowship of the Spirit, if any affection and mercy, fulfill my joy by being like-minded, having the same love, being of one accord, of one mind. Let nothing be done through selfish ambition or conceit, but in lowliness of mind let each esteem others better than himself.

PHILIPPIANS 2:1–3 NKJV

For though the LORD is exalted, yet He regards the lowly, but the haughty He knows from afar.

PSALM 138:6 NASB

He mocks proud mockers but gives grace to the humble.

PROVERBS 3:34 NIV

"Therefore whoever humbles himself as this little child is the greatest in the kingdom of heaven."

MATTHEW 18:4 NKJV

Humble yourselves in the presence of the Lord, and He will exalt you.

JAMES 4:10 NASB

Heavenly Father,

I pray that I will be humble.
Thank You for showing me what true humility is.
I want to follow Your example
and be known as a person of meekness.
Amen.

Joy

It seems like everyone's looking for happiness these days—from money, possessions, sex. . .you name it. But any pleasure that those things bring is short-lived.

True joy, however, is the deep-down, long-lasting satisfaction of a right relationship with God, the source of all good things. You can experience His gift of joy today and every day. Just don't keep it to yourself—be sure to spread it to others around you. They're probably looking for some!

Dear brothers and sisters, whenever trouble comes your way, let it be an opportunity for joy.

JAMES 1:2 NLT

Now may the God of hope fill you with all joy and peace in believing, that you may abound in hope by the power of the Holy Spirit.

ROMANS 15:13 NKJV

Grief can take care of itself,
but to get the full value of a joy
you must have somebody
to divide it with.

MARK TWAIN

"Truly, truly, I say to you, that you will weep and lament, but the world will rejoice; you will grieve, but your grief will be turned into joy."

JOHN 16:20 NASB

Speaking to yourselves in psalms and hymns and spiritual songs, singing and making melody in your heart to the Lord.

EPHESIANS 5:19 KJV

The LORD is my strength and my shield; my heart trusted in Him, and I am helped; therefore my heart greatly rejoices, and with my song I will praise Him.

PSALM 28:7 NKJV

My lips shall greatly rejoice when I sing to You, and my soul, which You have redeemed.

PSALM 71:23 NKJV

"You will go out in joy and be led forth in peace; the mountains and hills will burst into song before you, and all the trees of the field will clap their hands."

ISAIAH 55:12 NIV

Rejoicing in hope, persevering in tribulation, devoted to prayer. . .

ROMANS 12:12 NASB

"You have made known to me the ways of life; You will make me full of gladness with Your presence."

ACTS 2:28 NASB

Those who plant in tears will harvest with shouts of joy. They weep as they go to plant their seed, but they sing as they return with the harvest.

PSALM 126:5–6 NLT

"These things I have spoken to you, that My joy may remain in you, and that your joy may be full."

JOHN 15:11 NKJV

"Then shall the virgin rejoice in the dance, and the young men and the old, together; for I will turn their mourning to joy, will comfort them, and make them rejoice rather than sorrow."

JEREMIAH 31:13 NKJV

"He will yet fill your mouth with laughter and your lips with shouting."

JOB 8:21 NASB

But let all those that put their trust in thee rejoice: let them ever shout for joy, because thou defendest them: let them also that love thy name be joyful in thee.

PSALM 5:11 KJV

I will rejoice greatly in the LORD, my soul will exult in my God; for He has clothed me with garments of salvation, He has wrapped me with a robe of righteousness, as a bridegroom decks himself with a garland, and as a bride adorns herself with her jewels.

ISAIAH 61:10 NASB

"Until now you have asked for nothing in My name; ask and you will receive, so that your joy may be made full."

JOHN 16:24 NASB

You will show me the way of life, granting me the joy of your presence and the pleasures of living with you forever.

PSALM 16:11 NLT

"Rejoice in that day and leap for joy! For indeed your reward is great in heaven, for in like manner their fathers did to the prophets."

LUKE 6:23 NKJV

"But now I come to You; and these things I speak in the world so that they may have My joy made full in themselves."

JOHN 17:13 NASB

Rejoice in the LORD and be glad, you righteous; sing, all you who are upright in heart!

PSALM 32:11 NIV

Rejoice in the Lord always. Again I will say, rejoice!

PHILIPPIANS 4:4 NKJV

So the ransomed of the LORD shall return, and come to Zion with singing, with everlasting joy on their heads. They shall obtain joy and gladness; sorrow and sighing shall flee away.

ISAIAH 51:11 NKJV

Rejoice evermore. . . . In every thing give thanks: for this is the will of God in Christ Jesus concerning you.

1 THESSALONIANS 5:16, 18 KJV

Shout joyfully to the LORD,
all the earth.
Serve the LORD with gladness;
come before Him with joyful singing.

PSALM 100:1–2 NASB

A cheerful heart is good medicine, but a crushed spirit
dries up the bones.

PROVERBS 17:22 NIV

Today

I will focus on all of the great things
You've done for me, Lord.
Thank You for the way You provide for me,
for the friends You've given to me,
and most of all, for giving Your Son.
Help me to show joy on my face,
so that others around me will experience joy, too.
Amen.

Justice

Maybe you've seen an accused person on the television news, saying, "I demand that justice be served!" Here's a hint for you: Don't ever say that to God. His standards are so high that "justice" for us would be a very painful thing. Thankfully, God is not only just but merciful—that's why Jesus came to pay the price for our sins. God exemplifies justice to us and commands that we be just with each other. That's how to serve justice!

"You shall do no injustice in judgment. You shall not be partial to the poor, nor honor the person of the mighty. In righteousness you shall judge your neighbor."

LEVITICUS 19:15 NKJV

Never look for righteousness
in the other person,
but never cease to be righteous yourself.
We are always looking for justice,
yet the essence of the teaching
of the Sermon on the Mount is—
never look for justice,
but never cease to give it.

OSWALD CHAMBERS

"Do not judge according to appearance, but judge with righteous judgment."

JOHN 7:24 NASB

He will judge the world with justice and rule the nations with fairness.

PSALM 9:8 NLT

"You shall not pervert justice; you shall not show partiality, nor take a bribe, for a bribe blinds the eyes of the wise and twists the words of the righteous. You shall follow what is altogether just, that you may live and inherit the land which the LORD your God is giving you."

DEUTERONOMY 16:19–20 NKJV

[Jesus] whom God displayed publicly as a propitiation in His blood through faith. This was to demonstrate His righteousness, because in the forbearance of God He passed over the sins previously committed.

ROMANS 3:25 NASB

He will bring forth your righteousness as the light and your judgment as the noonday.

PSALM 37:6 NASB

And that no man transgress and defraud his brother in the matter because the Lord is the avenger in all these things, just as we also told you before and solemnly warned you. For God has not called us for the purpose of impurity, but in sanctification. So, he who rejects this is not rejecting man but the God who gives His Holy Spirit to you.

1 THESSALONIANS 4:6–8 NASB

"Thus says the LORD: 'Execute judgment and righteousness, and deliver the plundered out of the hand of the oppressor. Do no wrong and do no violence to the stranger, the fatherless, or the widow, nor shed innocent blood in this place.'"

JEREMIAH 22:3 NKJV

He loveth righteousness and judgment: the earth is full of the goodness of the LORD.

PSALM 33:5 KJV

"Learn to do good; seek justice, reprove the ruthless, defend the orphan, plead for the widow."

ISAIAH 1:17 NASB

"A bruised reed He will not break, and smoking flax He will not quench, till He sends forth justice to victory."

MATTHEW 12:20 NKJV

Hate evil, love good, and establish justice in the gate!

AMOS 5:15 NASB

Justice is a joy to the godly, but it causes dismay among evildoers.

PROVERBS 21:15 NLT

Thus speaketh the LORD of hosts, saying, Execute true judgment, and shew mercy and compassions every man to his brother.

ZECHARIAH 7:9 KJV

Blessed are those who keep justice, and he who does righteousness at all times!

PSALM 106:3 NKJV

The godly know the rights of the poor; the wicked don't care to know.

PROVERBS 29:7 NLT

"Does our law condemn anyone without first hearing him to find out what he is doing?"

JOHN 7:51 NIV

"I will betroth you to Me forever; yes, I will betroth you to Me in righteousness and justice, in lovingkindness and mercy."

HOSEA 2:19 NKJV

For the LORD is a God of justice.
Blessed are all who wait for him!

ISAIAH 30:18 NIV

"O Jacob My servant, do not fear," declares the LORD, "for I am with you. For I will make a full end of all the nations where I have driven you, yet I will not make a full end of you; but I will correct you properly and by no means leave you unpunished."

JEREMIAH 46:28 NASB

It is well with the man who is gracious and lends; he will maintain his cause in judgment.

PSALM 112:5 NASB

Moreover I saw under the sun: In the place of judgment, wickedness was there; and in the place of righteousness, iniquity was there. I said in my heart, "God shall judge the righteous and the wicked, for there is a time there for every purpose and for every work."

ECCLESIASTES 3:16–17 NKJV

"If there is a dispute between men. . .they come to court, that the judges may judge them, and they justify the righteous and condemn the wicked."

DEUTERONOMY 25:1 NKJV

But if ye had known what this meaneth, I will have mercy, and not sacrifice, ye would not have condemned the guiltless.

MATTHEW 12:7 KJV

Thus says the LORD, "Preserve justice and do righteousness, for My salvation is about to come and My righteousness to be revealed."

ISAIAH 56:1 NASB

"You shall not circulate a false report. Do not put your hand with the wicked to be an unrighteous witness. You shall not follow a crowd to do evil; nor shall you testify in a dispute so as to turn aside after many to pervert justice. You shall not show partiality to a poor man in his dispute."

EXODUS 23:1–3 NKJV

Lord God,
*in a world where very little seems fair,
I thank You that I can count on You to be fair and just.
Thank You, too, for not giving me what I deserve,
but for showing me mercy.
Amen.*

Labor

In some circles, it's cool to make fun of work and to try to get away with as little as possible. But that attitude is 180 degrees out of phase with God's. Work is an honorable, beneficial thing that, frankly, can keep us out of trouble.

Sure, some jobs can be mundane at times, but remember the One for whom you are ultimately working—it's not just your boss keeping an eye on your efforts. Be thankful for the job God gave you and work to do the best that you can for His glory.

For the LORD your God will bless you in all your harvest and in all the work of your hands, and your joy will be complete.

DEUTERONOMY 16:15 NIV

Therefore, my beloved brethren, be steadfast, immovable, always abounding in the work of the Lord, knowing that your labor is not in vain in the Lord.

1 CORINTHIANS 15:58 NKJV

The Son of God
reveals Himself in me,
and I serve Him in
the ordinary ways of life
out of devotion to Him.

OSWALD CHAMBERS

When you shall eat of the fruit of your hands, you will be happy and it will be well with you.

PSALM 128:2 NASB

Hard work means prosperity; only fools idle away their time.

PROVERBS 12:11 NLT

"But you, be strong and do not let your hands be weak, for your work shall be rewarded!"

2 CHRONICLES 15:7 NKJV

Do not love sleep, lest you come to poverty; open your eyes, and you will be satisfied with bread.

PROVERBS 20:13 NKJV

For even when we were with you, we used to give you this order: if anyone is not willing to work, then he is not to eat, either.

2 THESSALONIANS 3:10 NASB

Whatsoever thy hand findeth to do, do it with thy might; for there is no work, nor device, nor knowledge, nor wisdom, in the grave, whither thou goest.

ECCLESIASTES 9:10 KJV

Let the favor of the Lord our God be upon us; and confirm for us the work of our hands; yes, confirm the work of our hands.

PSALM 90:17 NASB

He who has been stealing must steal no longer, but must work, doing something useful with his own hands, that he may have something to share with those in need.

EPHESIANS 4:28 NIV

"For the LORD your God has blessed you in all that you have done; He has known your wanderings through this great wilderness. These forty years the LORD your God has been with you; you have not lacked a thing."

DEUTERONOMY 2:7 NASB

He becometh poor that dealeth with a slack hand: but the hand of the diligent maketh rich.

PROVERBS 10:4 KJV

Now he who plants and he who waters are one, and each one will receive his own reward according to his own labor.

1 CORINTHIANS 3:8 NKJV

Then I heard a voice from heaven saying to me, "Write: 'Blessed are the dead who die in the Lord from now on.'" "Yes," says the Spirit, "that they may rest from their labors, and their works follow them."

REVELATION 14:13 NKJV

Make it your ambition to lead a quiet life and attend to your own business and work with your hands, just as we commanded you, so that you will behave properly toward outsiders and not be in any need.

1 THESSALONIANS 4:11–12 NASB

Do you see a man skilled in his work? He will stand before kings; He will not stand before obscure men.

PROVERBS 22:29 NASB

"Six days you shall labor and do all your work, but the seventh day is the Sabbath of the LORD your God. In it you shall do no work: you, nor your son, nor your daughter, nor your male servant, nor your female servant, nor your cattle, nor your stranger who is within your gates."

EXODUS 20:9–10 NKJV

Dear God,

I want to put forth my best effort in my job.
Remind me that I'm not only working for money
or to please my boss, but for You.
Thank You for giving me my job.
Amen.

Loving God

Remember the time Jesus asked Peter, "Do you love Me?" Peter's answer, in modern paraphrase, was, "Yeah, Lord, I love you." Jesus responded, "Feed My sheep," then repeated the exchange two more times. Peter seemed hurt that Jesus would ask him the same question three times, implying that Peter didn't really love Jesus.

It's easy to say that we love God, but it is so much more significant to show that we love Him. Tell God through your actions how much He means to you and how thankful you are that He is your God.

"But from there you will seek the LORD your God, and you will find Him if you seek Him with all your heart and with all your soul."

DEUTERONOMY 4:29 NKJV

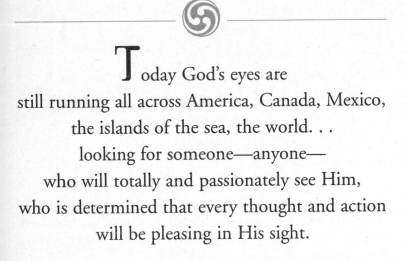

Today God's eyes are
still running all across America, Canada, Mexico,
the islands of the sea, the world. . .
looking for someone—anyone—
who will totally and passionately see Him,
who is determined that every thought and action
will be pleasing in His sight.

JIM CYMBALA

But if anyone loves God, he is known by Him.

1 CORINTHIANS 8:3 NASB

The LORD watches over all who love him, but all the wicked he will destroy.

PSALM 145:20 NIV

"So be very careful to love the LORD your God."

JOSHUA 23:11 NLT

Do not love the world or the things in the world. If anyone loves the world, the love of the Father is not in him.

1 JOHN 2:15 NKJV

And we know that God causes all things to work together for good to those who love God, to those who are called according to His purpose.

ROMANS 8:28 NASB

"I love those who love me; and those who diligently seek me will find me."

PROVERBS 8:17 NASB

Jesus said unto them, If God were your Father, ye would love me: for I proceeded forth and came from God; neither came I of myself, but he sent me.

JOHN 8:42 KJV

Therefore be imitators of God as dear children. And walk in love, as Christ also has loved us and given Himself for us, an offering and a sacrifice to God for a sweet-smelling aroma.

EPHESIANS 5:1–2 NKJV

"And you shall love the LORD your God with all your heart, with all your soul, with all your mind, and with all your strength. This is the first commandment."

MARK 12:30 NKJV

For God is not unjust so as to forget your work and the love which you have shown toward His name, in having ministered and in still ministering to the saints.

HEBREWS 6:10 NASB

"You shall love the LORD your God with all your heart, with all your soul, and with all your strength. And these words which I command you today shall be in your heart."

DEUTERONOMY 6:5–6 NKJV

And we have known and believed the love that God has for us. God is love, and he who abides in love abides in God, and God in him. Love has been perfected among us in this: that we may have boldness in the day of judgment; because as He is, so are we in this world. There is no fear in love; but perfect love casts out fear, because fear involves torment. But he who fears has not been made perfect in love. We love Him because He first loved us.

1 JOHN 4:16–19 NKJV

So that Christ may dwell in your hearts through faith; and that you, being rooted and grounded in love, may be able to comprehend with all the saints what is the breadth and length and height and depth, and to know the love of Christ which surpasses knowledge, that you may be filled up to all the fullness of God.

EPHESIANS 3:17–19 NASB

"Those who obey my commandments are the ones who love me. And because they love me, my Father will love them, and I will love them. And I will reveal myself to each one of them."

JOHN 14:21 NLT

Keep yourselves in God's love as you wait for the mercy of our Lord Jesus Christ to bring you to eternal life.

JUDE 21 NIV

Lord Jesus,
I love You.
Words are so easy to speak,
but I want You to know they come from my heart.
I want to show You how much I love You
and how thankful I am that You're my Lord.
You are the source of my life,
and I will always love and serve You.
Amen.

Obedience

We send our dogs to "obedience school"—but maybe we should send ourselves. There's just something about submitting to authority that grates on our selfish human natures. But just like Rover at "school," we can earn rewards for obedience, whether from our parents, our government, or most importantly, our God. Demonstrate your love for Him by obeying Him—remember, Jesus said, "If you will obey my commands, you will remain in my love."

If ye keep my commandments, ye shall abide in my love; even as I have kept my Father's commandments, and abide in his love.

JOHN 15:10 KJV

The things which you learned and received and heard and saw in me, these do, and the God of peace will be with you.

PHILIPPIANS 4:9 NKJV

Obey your leaders and submit to their authority. They keep watch over you as men who must give an account. Obey them so that their work will be a joy, not a burden, for that would be of no advantage to you.

HEBREWS 13:17 NIV

"Not everyone who says to Me, 'Lord, Lord,' will enter the kingdom of heaven, but he who does the will of My Father who is in heaven will enter."

MATTHEW 7:21 NASB

Samuel said, "Has the LORD as much delight in burnt offerings and sacrifices as in obeying the voice of the LORD? Behold, to obey is better than sacrifice, and to heed than the fat of rams."

1 SAMUEL 15:22 NASB

"If you consent and obey, you will eat the best of the land."

ISAIAH 1:19 NASB

"If they hear and serve Him, they will end their days in prosperity and their years in pleasures."

JOB 36:11 NASB

Always remember that
when you came to Christ,
you became His responsibility.
Your part is explicit obedience
to everything He tells you to do.
His part is covering all the consequences
that result from your obedience.

RAY ORTLUND

And the person who keeps all of the laws except one is as guilty as the person who has broken all of God's laws.

JAMES 2:10 NLT

"The LORD your God will make you abound in all the work of your hand, in the fruit of your body, in the increase of your livestock, and in the produce of your land for good. For the LORD will again rejoice over you for good as He rejoiced over your fathers, if you obey the voice of the LORD your God, to keep His commandments and His statutes which are written in this Book of the Law, and if you turn to the LORD your God with all your heart and with all your soul."

DEUTERONOMY 30:9–10 NKJV

Let us hear the conclusion of the whole matter: Fear God and keep His commandments, for this is man's all.

ECCLESIASTES 12:13 NKJV

All the paths of the LORD are mercy and truth unto such as keep his covenant and his testimonies.

PSALM 25:10 KJV

By this we know that we have come to know Him, if we keep His commandments. The one who says, "I have come to know Him," and does not keep His commandments, is a liar, and the truth is not in him; but whoever keeps His word, in him the love of God has truly been perfected. By this we know that we are in Him: the one who says he abides in Him ought himself to walk in the same manner as He walked.

1 JOHN 2:3–6 NASB

"Oh, that they had such a heart in them that they would fear Me and always keep all My commandments, that it might be well with them and with their children forever!"

DEUTERONOMY 5:29 NKJV

My son, do not forget my teaching, but keep my commands in your heart, for they will prolong your life many years and bring you prosperity.

PROVERBS 3:1–2 NIV

For not the hearers of the law are just in the sight of God, but the doers of the law will be justified.

ROMANS 2:13 NKJV

And the world is passing away, and the lust of it; but he who does the will of God abides forever.

1 JOHN 2:17 NKJV

Furthermore,
we had earthly fathers to discipline us,
and we respected them;
shall we not much rather be subject to
the Father of spirits, and live?

HEBREWS 12:9 NASB

And now, just as you accepted Christ Jesus as your Lord, you must continue to live in obedience to him. Let your roots grow down into him and draw up nourishment from him, so you will grow in faith, strong and vigorous in the truth you were taught. Let your lives overflow with thanksgiving for all he has done.

COLOSSIANS 2:6–7 NLT

Submit yourselves for the Lord's sake to every human institution, whether to a king as the one in authority, or to governors as sent by him for the punishment of evildoers and the praise of those who do right.

1 PETER 2:13–14 NASB

But prove yourselves doers of the word, and not merely hearers who delude themselves. For if anyone is a hearer of the word and not a doer, he is like a man who looks at his natural face in a mirror; for once he has looked at himself and gone away, he has immediately forgotten what kind of person he was. But one who looks intently at the perfect law, the law of liberty, and abides by it, not having become a forgetful hearer but an effectual doer, this man will be blessed in what he does.

JAMES 1:22–25 NASB

"Now that you know these things, you will be blessed if you do them."

JOHN 13:17 NIV

But He said, "More than that, blessed are those who hear the word of God and keep it!"

LUKE 11:28 NKJV

In that I command thee this day to love the LORD thy God, to walk in his ways, and to keep his commandments and his statutes and his judgments, that thou mayest live and multiply: and the LORD thy God shall bless thee in the land whither thou goest to possess it.

DEUTERONOMY 30:16 KJV

Heavenly Father,
teach me to obey.
I want to follow Your way,
even when I may not understand why
You're taking me through certain situations.
Thank You for the authorities in my life.
Please remind me that in obeying them
I am obeying You.
Amen.

Patience

You've probably heard that "patience is a virtue." Virtuous or not, what exactly is patience?

For the Christian, patience is more than merely waiting for something to occur; it's a waiting coupled with the right heart attitude—a conscious belief that God is working out His purpose in our lives, no matter how the immediate circumstances appear. Sure, it's easier said than done—but developing patience is one of the best investments you'll ever make in yourself.

He who is slow to anger is better than the mighty, and he who rules his spirit than he who takes a city.

PROVERBS 16:32 NKJV

And so, having patiently waited, he obtained the promise.

HEBREWS 6:15 NASB

] choose patience. . . .
I will overlook the
inconveniences of the world.
Instead of cursing the one who takes my place,
I'll invite him to do so.
Rather than complain that the wait is too long,
I will thank God for a moment to pray.

MAX LUCADO

Be still before the LORD and wait patiently for him; do not fret when men succeed in their ways, when they carry out their wicked schemes. . . . For evil men will be cut off, but those who hope in the LORD will inherit the land.

PSALM 37:7, 9 NIV

Be humble and gentle. Be patient with each other, making allowance for each other's faults because of your love.

EPHESIANS 4:2 NLT

I waited patiently for the LORD; and He inclined to me, and heard my cry.

PSALM 40:1 NKJV

The testing of your faith produces endurance. And let endurance have its perfect result, so that you may be perfect and complete, lacking in nothing.

JAMES 1:3–4 NASB

That ye be not slothful, but followers of them who through faith and patience inherit the promises.

HEBREWS 6:12 KJV

This calls for patient endurance on the part of the saints who obey God's commandments and remain faithful to Jesus.

REVELATION 14:12 NIV

Be glad for all God is planning for you. Be patient in trouble, and always be prayerful.

ROMANS 12:12 NLT

The end of a thing is better than its beginning; the patient in spirit is better than the proud in spirit.

ECCLESIASTES 7:8 NKJV

The discretion of a man makes him slow to anger, and his glory is to overlook a transgression.

PROVERBS 19:11 NKJV

Those who control their anger have great understanding; those with a hasty temper will make mistakes.

PROVERBS 14:29 NLT

Now we exhort you, brethren, warn those who are unruly, comfort the fainthearted, uphold the weak, be patient with all.

1 THESSALONIANS 5:14 NKJV

Therefore be patient, brethren, until the coming of the Lord. The farmer waits for the precious produce of the soil, being patient about it, until it gets the early and late rains. You too be patient; strengthen your hearts, for the coming of the Lord is near.

JAMES 5:7–8 NASB

Wait on the LORD: be of good courage, and he shall strengthen thine heart: wait, I say, on the LORD.

PSALM 27:14 KJV

Dear Lord,

please help me to slow down.
In a world where hurrying is the norm, teach me to wait.
I know that You have the best for me;
I want to be willing to wait for things in Your time.
Amen.

Peace

First day on the new job. . .car breakdown. . .big date Friday night. . .illness in the family. . . There is no shortage of anxiety in our fast-paced, stressful world. But God (that's a great phrase!) has provided peace so that we can rest in Him. God, and only God, can give us the strength and ability to survive, and even thrive among, the pressures of the world. It may be a cliché, but that doesn't make the following quote any less true: "No God, no peace. Know God, know peace."

Be anxious for nothing, but in everything by prayer and supplication, with thanksgiving, let your requests be made known to God; and the peace of God, which surpasses all understanding, will guard your hearts and minds through Christ Jesus.

PHILIPPIANS 4:6-7 NKJV

There is a way to inner peace,
but it isn't through our own sophistication,
abilities, talents, or internal makeup;
it is through God.

ROGER PALMS

For the mind set on the flesh is death, but the mind set on the Spirit is life and peace.

ROMANS 8:6 NASB

Consider the blameless, observe the upright; there is a future for the man of peace.

PSALM 37:37 NIV

Peace I leave with you, my peace I give unto you: not as the world giveth, give I unto you. Let not your heart be troubled, neither let it be afraid.

JOHN 14:27 KJV

"You will keep him in perfect peace, whose mind is stayed on You, because he trusts in You."

ISAIAH 26:3 NKJV

So then we pursue the things which make for peace and the building up of one another.

ROMANS 14:19 NASB

He who dwells in the shelter of the Most High will abide in the shadow of the Almighty.

PSALM 91:1 NASB

For the Scriptures say, "If you want a happy life and good days, keep your tongue from speaking evil, and keep your lips from telling lies. Turn away from evil and do good. Work hard at living in peace with others."

1 PETER 3:10–11 NLT

"Let not your heart be troubled; you believe in God, believe also in Me."

JOHN 14:1 NKJV

Therefore, having been justified by faith, we have peace with God through our Lord Jesus Christ.

ROMANS 5:1 NKJV

"Glory to God in the highest, and on earth peace among men with whom He is pleased."

LUKE 2:14 NASB

For the Kingdom of God is not a matter of what we eat or drink, but of living a life of goodness and peace and joy in the Holy Spirit.

ROMANS 14:17 NLT

Be at peace among yourselves.

1 THESSALONIANS 5:13 NKJV

I will lie down and sleep in peace, for you alone, O LORD, make me dwell in safety.

PSALM 4:8 NIV

Being diligent to preserve the unity of the Spirit in the bond of peace. . .

EPHESIANS 4:3 NASB

Surely He shall deliver you from the snare of the fowler and from the perilous pestilence. He shall cover you with His feathers, and under His wings you shall take refuge; His truth shall be your shield and buckler. You shall not be afraid of the terror by night, nor of the arrow that flies by day, nor of the pestilence that walks in darkness, nor of the destruction that lays waste at noonday.

PSALM 91:3–6 NKJV

Turn from evil and do good; seek peace and pursue it.

PSALM 34:14 NIV

And let the peace of God rule in your hearts, to which also you were called in one body; and be thankful.

COLOSSIANS 3:15 NKJV

Have not I commanded thee? Be strong and of a good courage; be not afraid, neither be thou dismayed: for the LORD thy God is with thee whithersoever thou goest.

JOSHUA 1:9 KJV

Do your part to live in peace with everyone, as much as possible.

ROMANS 12:18 NLT

A thousand may fall at your side, and ten thousand at your right hand; but it shall not come near you. Only with your eyes shall you look, and see the reward of the wicked. Because you have made the LORD, who is my refuge, even the Most High, your dwelling place, no evil shall befall you, nor shall any plague come near your dwelling.

PSALM 91:7–10 NKJV

God has called us to peace.

1 CORINTHIANS 7:15 NASB

Now the fruit of righteousness is sown in peace by those who make peace.

JAMES 3:18 NKJV

First of all, then, I urge that entreaties and prayers, petitions and thanksgivings, be made on behalf of all men, for kings and all who are in authority, so that we may lead a tranquil and quiet life in all godliness and dignity.

1 TIMOTHY 2:1–2 NASB

The LORD will give strength to His people; the LORD will bless His people with peace.

PSALM 29:11 NKJV

Blessed are the peacemakers,
for they shall be called sons of God."

MATTHEW 5:9 NASB

Deceit is in the heart of them that imagine evil: but to the counsellors of peace is joy.

PROVERBS 12:20 KJV

Those who love Your law have great peace, and nothing causes them to stumble.

PSALM 119:165 NASB

Make every effort to live in peace with all men and to be holy; without holiness no one will see the Lord.

HEBREWS 12:14 NIV

Now may the Lord of peace Himself give you peace always in every way. The Lord be with you all.

2 THESSALONIANS 3:16 NKJV

Lord Jesus,
thank You for giving me peace
when all of life goes haywire.
Remind me not to get caught up in the hubbub
but to quietly rest in You.
Amen.

Perseverance

A handful of people are born with tremendous gifts—athletic skills, musical talents, intellectual abilities—and seem destined to succeed. But what about the rest of us—the normal people who test out average? The key to our success is perseverance, hard work in the face of every obstacle—that quality that previous generations called "stick-to-itiveness." Perseverance is a great trait to develop in life—and especially in our spiritual lives. God wants marathon runners, not sprinters!

I can do all things through Christ who strengthens me.

PHILIPPIANS 4:13 NKJV

To those who by persistence in doing good seek glory, honor and immortality, he will give eternal life.

ROMANS 2:7 NIV

I think and think
for months and years,
ninety-nine times, the conclusion is false.
The hundredth time I am right.

ALBERT EINSTEIN

Yet I am not ashamed, because I know whom I have believed, and am convinced that he is able to guard what I have entrusted to him for that day. What you heard from me, keep as the pattern of sound teaching, with faith and love in Christ Jesus.

2 TIMOTHY 1:12–13 NIV

Then Jesus said to those Jews who believed Him, "If you abide in My word, you are My disciples indeed."

JOHN 8:31 NKJV

Here is the perseverance of the saints who keep the commandments of God and their faith in Jesus.

REVELATION 14:12 NASB

God blesses the people who patiently endure testing. Afterward they will receive the crown of life that God has promised to those who love him.

JAMES 1:12 NLT

You therefore must endure hardship as a good soldier of Jesus Christ.

2 TIMOTHY 2:3 NKJV

Whatever you do, do your work heartily, as for the Lord rather than for men, knowing that from the Lord you will receive the reward of the inheritance. It is the Lord Christ whom you serve.

COLOSSIANS 3:23–24 NASB

And let us not be weary in well doing: for in due season we shall reap, if we faint not.

GALATIANS 6:9 KJV

And not only that, but we also glory in tribulations, knowing that tribulation produces perseverance; and perseverance, character; and character, hope.

ROMANS 5:3–4 NKJV

Let us hold fast the confession of our hope without wavering, for He who promised is faithful.

HEBREWS 10:23 NASB

May the Lord direct your hearts into God's love and Christ's perseverance.

2 THESSALONIANS 3:5 NIV

You therefore, beloved, since you know this beforehand, beware lest you also fall from your own steadfastness, being led away with the error of the wicked.

2 PETER 3:17 NKJV

For we have become partakers of Christ, if we hold fast the beginning of our assurance firm until the end.

HEBREWS 3:14 NASB

"I will invite everyone who is victorious to sit with me on my throne, just as I was victorious and sat with my Father on his throne."

REVELATION 3:21 NLT

Stand fast therefore in the liberty by which Christ has made us free, and do not be entangled again with a yoke of bondage.

GALATIANS 5:1 NKJV

Therefore we also, since we are surrounded by so great a cloud of witnesses, let us lay aside every weight, and the sin which so easily ensnares us, and let us run with endurance the race that is set before us, looking unto Jesus, the author and finisher of our faith, who for the joy that was set before Him endured the cross, despising the shame, and has sat down at the right hand of the throne of God.

HEBREWS 12:1–2 NKJV

Wherefore take unto you the whole armour of God, that ye may be able to withstand in the evil day, and having done all, to stand.

EPHESIANS 6:13 KJV

I have fought a good fight, I have finished my course, I have kept the faith: Henceforth there is laid up for me a crown of righteousness, which the Lord, the righteous judge, shall give me at that day: and not to me only, but unto all them also that love his appearing.

2 TIMOTHY 4:7–8 KJV

Everyone who competes in the games exercises self-control in all things. They then do it to receive a perishable wreath, but we an imperishable. Therefore I run in such a way, as not without aim; I box in such a way, as not beating the air; but I discipline my body and make it my slave, so that, after I have preached to others, I myself will not be disqualified.

1 CORINTHIANS 9:25–27 NASB

Father,

sometimes I am tempted to just give up.
But You have awesome plans in store for me if
I will just remember to lean on You
for the strength I need.
Thank You for the blessings You have promised me
as I "run the race."
Amen.

Physical Care

True or false: Working out makes you a better person.

Exercise may make you a better person physically—you'll probably look better and feel better about yourself. It is wise to take care of the body that God gave you. But even though physical care is necessary, it's not nearly as important as spiritual care—so make sure you've got your priorities in the proper order. Running a five-minute mile is great—but spending five minutes in God's Word is even better.

For bodily discipline is only of little profit, but godliness is profitable for all things, since it holds promise for the present life and also for the life to come.

1 TIMOTHY 4:8 NASB

Do you not know that your body is a temple of the Holy Spirit, who is in you, whom you have received from God? You are not your own; you were bought at a price. Therefore honor God with your body.

1 CORINTHIANS 6:19–20 NIV

My deeds will not be
measured by my youthful appearance,
but by the concern lines on my forehead
and the laugh lines around my mouth.

ERMA BOMBECK

Beloved, I pray that in all respects you may prosper and be in good health, just as your soul prospers.

3 JOHN 2 NASB

"Do not fear those who kill the body but are unable to kill the soul; but rather fear Him who is able to destroy both soul and body in hell."

MATTHEW 10:28 NASB

You do not know what will happen tomorrow. For what is your life? It is even a vapor that appears for a little time and then vanishes away. Instead you ought to say, "If the Lord wills, we shall live and do this or that."

JAMES 4:14–15 NKJV

And so, dear brothers and sisters, I plead with you to give your bodies to God. Let them be a living and holy sacrifice—the kind he will accept. When you think of what he has done for you, is this too much to ask? Don't copy the behavior and customs of this world, but let God transform you into a new person by changing the way you think. Then you will know what God wants you to do, and you will know how good and pleasing and perfect his will really is. As God's messenger, I give each of you this warning: Be honest in your estimate of yourselves, measuring your value by how much faith God has given you.

ROMANS 12:1–3 NLT

Charm is deceitful and beauty is passing, but a woman who fears the LORD, she shall be praised.

PROVERBS 31:30 NKJV

"Do not judge according to appearance, but judge with righteous judgment."

JOHN 7:24 NKJV

But the LORD said unto Samuel, Look not on his countenance, or on the height of his stature; because I have refused him: for the LORD seeth not as man seeth; for man looketh on the outward appearance, but the LORD looketh on the heart.

1 SAMUEL 16:7 KJV

Therefore, from now on, we regard no one according to the flesh. Even though we have known Christ according to the flesh, yet now we know Him thus no longer. Therefore, if anyone is in Christ, he is a new creation; old things have passed away; behold, all things have become new.

2 CORINTHIANS 5:16–17 NKJV

Likewise, I want women to adorn themselves with proper clothing, modestly and discreetly, not with braided hair and gold or pearls or costly garments, but rather by means of good works, as is proper for women making a claim to godliness.

1 TIMOTHY 2:9–10 NASB

If you show special attention to the man wearing fine clothes and say, "Here's a good seat for you," but say to the poor man, "You stand there" or "Sit on the floor by my feet," have you not discriminated among yourselves and become judges with evil thoughts?

JAMES 2:3–4 NIV

Dear Lord,

I know that I am the temple of Your Holy Spirit.
I want to take care of my body
and not do anything that will harm it.
Please help me pay attention to what I eat and drink
and to keep myself fit.
I want to be a living sacrifice for You.
Amen.

Prayer

Sometimes the whole concept is hard to grasp: the holy, all-powerful God actually wants us to talk to Him. It's called prayer.

Although God knows what you will say even before you do, He still waits for you to enter His presence in prayer. No request is too large (or too small!) to take before Him. God loves you and wants to answer your prayers. Have a hard time believing that? Then read the following verses!

Therefore I want the men in every place to pray, lifting up holy hands, without wrath and dissension.

1 TIMOTHY 2:8 NASB

"If you sinful people know how to give good gifts to your children, how much more will your heavenly Father give good gifts to those who ask him."

MATTHEW 7:11 NLT

Prayer is in very deed
the pulse of the spiritual life.
It is the great means of bringing to
minister and people the blessing
and power of heaven.
Persevering and believing prayer means
a strong and an abundant life.

ANDREW MURRAY

In the same way the Spirit also helps our weakness; for we do not know how to pray as we should, but the Spirit Himself intercedes for us with groanings too deep for words.

ROMANS 8:26 NASB

The LORD is near to all who call upon Him, to all who call upon Him in truth.

PSALM 145:18 NKJV

Then shall ye call upon me, and ye shall go and pray unto me, and I will hearken unto you.

JEREMIAH 29:12 KJV

He shall call upon Me, and I will answer him; I will be with him in trouble; I will deliver him and honor him.

PSALM 91:15 NKJV

"Until now you have asked for nothing in My name; ask and you will receive, so that your joy may be made full."

JOHN 16:24 NASB

The LORD detests the sacrifice of the wicked, but the prayer of the upright pleases him.

PROVERBS 15:8 NIV

"We will give ourselves continually to prayer and to the ministry of the word."

ACTS 6:4 NKJV

"It will also come to pass that before they call, I will answer; and while they are still speaking, I will hear."

ISAIAH 65:24 NASB

For the people shall dwell in Zion at Jerusalem; you shall weep no more. He will be very gracious to you at the sound of your cry; when He hears it, He will answer you.

ISAIAH 30:19 NKJV

Morning, noon, and night I plead aloud in my distress, and the LORD hears my voice.

PSALM 55:17 NLT

"Ask, and it will be given to you; seek, and you will find; knock, and it will be opened to you."

MATTHEW 7:7 NKJV

Be anxious for nothing, but in everything by prayer and supplication with thanksgiving let your requests be made known to God. And the peace of God, which surpasses all comprehension, will guard your hearts and your minds in Christ Jesus.

PHILIPPIANS 4:6–7 NASB

For this shall every one that is godly pray unto thee in a time when thou mayest be found: surely in the floods of great waters they shall not come nigh unto him.

PSALM 32:6 KJV

Therefore, confess your sins to one another, and pray for one another so that you may be healed. The effective prayer of a righteous man can accomplish much.

JAMES 5:16 NASB

"Again I say to you that if two of you agree on earth concerning anything that they ask, it will be done for them by My Father in heaven. For where two or three are gathered together in My name, I am there in the midst of them."

MATTHEW 18:19–20 NKJV

You will make your prayer to Him, He will hear you, and you will pay your vows.

JOB 22:27 NKJV

But I pray to you, O LORD, in the time of your favor; in your great love, O God, answer me with your sure salvation.

PSALM 69:13 NIV

Praying always with all prayer and supplication in the Spirit, being watchful to this end with all perseverance and supplication for all the saints.

EPHESIANS 6:18 NKJV

Rejoicing in hope,
persevering in tribulation,
devoted to prayer. . .

ROMANS 12:12 NASB

"Then he will pray to God, and He will accept him, that he may see His face with joy, and He may restore His righteousness to man."

JOB 33:26 NASB

O LORD, hear me as I pray; pay attention to my groaning. Listen to my cry for help, my King and my God, for I will never pray to anyone but you. Listen to my voice in the morning, LORD.

PSALM 5:1–3 NLT

"But when you pray, go away by yourself, shut the door behind you, and pray to your Father secretly. Then your Father, who knows all secrets, will reward you. When you pray, don't babble on and on as people of other religions do. They think their prayers are answered only by repeating their words again and again."

MATTHEW 6:6–7 NLT

What is the outcome then? I will pray with the spirit and I will pray with the mind also; I will sing with the spirit and I will sing with the mind also.

1 CORINTHIANS 14:15 NASB

I waited patiently for the LORD; and he inclined unto me, and heard my cry.

PSALM 40:1 KJV

Let us then approach the throne of grace with confidence, so that we may receive mercy and find grace to help us in our time of need.

HEBREWS 4:16 NIV

The prayer offered in faith will restore the one who is sick, and the Lord will raise him up, and if he has committed sins, they will be forgiven him.

JAMES 5:15 NASB

"And whatever things you ask in prayer, believing, you will receive."

MATTHEW 21:22 NKJV

Pray without ceasing; in everything give thanks; for this is God's will for you in Christ Jesus.

1 THESSALONIANS 5:17–18 NASB

Now this is the confidence that we have in Him, that if we ask anything according to His will, He hears us. And if we know that He hears us, whatever we ask, we know that we have the petitions that we have asked of Him.

1 JOHN 5:14–15 NKJV

If my people, which are called by my name, shall humble themselves, and pray, and seek my face, and turn from their wicked ways; then will I hear from heaven, and will forgive their sin, and will heal their land.

2 CHRONICLES 7:14 KJV

Dear God,

please make me a person of prayer.
I don't want to come to You
with only a list of wants and needs.
I want to come into Your presence,
thanking You for who You are
and for what You've done.
Teach me to not only talk to You
but to wait quietly for Your answer.
Amen.

Purity

In a sex-crazy world, purity seems like a horribly out-dated idea. You certainly won't find much support for it in movies, TV shows, or popular music. But the Christian faith is truly countercultural—and purity means a lot. Not only to God, either—what greater gift could a person give his or her future spouse than the gift of purity? When you choose to remain pure, you avoid the dangers of pregnancy, disease, and guilt, and you give yourself a much greater chance of having a long-lasting, happy marriage. Old-fashioned? Yes—but it works!

For all that is in the world—the lust of the flesh, the lust of the eyes, and the pride of life—is not of the Father but is of the world. And the world is passing away, and the lust of it; but he who does the will of God abides forever.

1 JOHN 2:16–17 NKJV

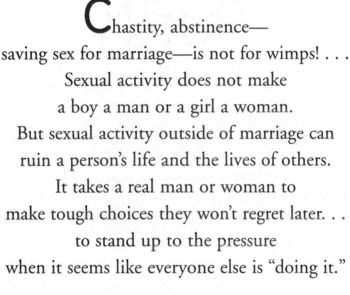

Chastity, abstinence—
saving sex for marriage—is not for wimps! . . .
Sexual activity does not make
a boy a man or a girl a woman.
But sexual activity outside of marriage can
ruin a person's life and the lives of others.
It takes a real man or woman to
make tough choices they won't regret later. . .
to stand up to the pressure
when it seems like everyone else is "doing it."

LINDA BARTLETT

But put on the Lord Jesus Christ, and make no provision for the flesh, to fulfill its lusts.

ROMANS 13:14 NKJV

Now concerning the things about which you wrote, it is good for a man not to touch a woman. But because of immoralities, each man is to have his own wife, and each woman is to have her own husband.

1 Corinthians 7:1–2 nasb

Do you not know that your bodies are members of Christ? Shall I then take away the members of Christ and make them members of a prostitute? May it never be! Or do you not know that the one who joins himself to a prostitute is one body with her? For He says, "The two shall become one flesh." But the one who joins himself to the Lord is one spirit with Him. Flee immorality. Every other sin that a man commits is outside the body, but the immoral man sins against his own body. Or do you not know that your body is a temple of the Holy Spirit who is in you, whom you have from God, and that you are not your own? For you have been bought with a price: therefore glorify God in your body.

1 Corinthians 6:15–20 nasb

Be imitators of God, therefore, as dearly loved children and live a life of love, just as Christ loved us and gave himself up for us as a fragrant offering and sacrifice to God. But among you there must not be even a hint of sexual immorality, or of any kind of impurity, or of greed, because these are improper for God's holy people.

Ephesians 5:1–3 niv

But I say unto you, That whosoever looketh on a woman to lust after her hath committed adultery with her already in his heart.

Matthew 5:28 kjv

For this is the will of God, your sanctification: that you should abstain from sexual immorality; that each of you should know how to possess his own vessel in sanctification and honor, not in passion of lust, like the Gentiles who do not know God. . . for God did not call us to uncleanness, but in holiness.

1 THESSALONIANS 4:3–5, 7 NKJV

So I advise you to live according to your new life in the Holy Spirit. Then you won't be doing what your sinful nature craves.

GALATIANS 5:16 NLT

The body is not meant for sexual immorality, but for the Lord, and the Lord for the body.

1 CORINTHIANS 6:13 NIV

Finally, brethren, whatever is true, whatever is honorable, whatever is right, whatever is pure, whatever is lovely, whatever is of good repute, if there is any excellence and if anything worthy of praise, dwell on these things.

PHILIPPIANS 4:8 NASB

"I have made a covenant with my eyes; why then should I look upon a young woman?"

JOB 31:1 NKJV

Therefore put to death your members which are on the earth: fornication, uncleanness, passion, evil desire, and covetousness, which is idolatry. Because of these things the wrath of God is coming upon the sons of disobedience.

COLOSSIANS 3:5–6 NKJV

Now those who belong to Christ Jesus have crucified the flesh with its passions and desires.

GALATIANS 5:24 NASB

Heavenly Father,

I pray for strength to remain pure.
With so many outside influences,
it could be easy to give in.
But I know that is not Your plan for my life—
You have something very special in store for me.
Help me to run from temptation.
Amen.

Relationships

Relationships is one of those multipurpose words. It can cover your friendships, your family ties, and your church connections. Those "relationships" are made up of special people who share your happiness and your pain. They're the people who laugh with you, listen to you when you need to talk, pray with you, encourage you, and support you through adversity. God knew that you would need that kind of support, so He gave you relationships. Thank Him for the ones He's brought into your life.

Now may the God who gives perseverance and encouragement grant you to be of the same mind with one another according to Christ Jesus.

ROMANS 15:5 NASB

"Honor your father and mother." This is the first of the Ten Commandments that ends with a promise. And this is the promise: If you honor your father and mother, "you will live a long life, full of blessing."

EPHESIANS 6:2–3 NLT

] cannot even imagine where I would be
today were it not for that handful
of friends who have given me a heart full of joy.
Let's face it—friends make life a lot more fun.

CHARLES SWINDOLL

For all the law is fulfilled in one word, even in this: "You shall love your neighbor as yourself."

GALATIANS 5:14 NKJV

Finally, all of you, live in harmony with one another; be sympathetic, love as brothers, be compassionate and humble.

1 PETER 3:8 NIV

If you really fulfill the royal law according to the Scripture, "You shall love your neighbor as yourself," you do well.

JAMES 2:8 NKJV

Anyone who hates his brother is a murderer, and you know that no murderer has eternal life in him.

1 JOHN 3:15 NIV

Though I speak with the tongues of men and of angels, and have not charity, I am become as sounding brass, or a tinkling cymbal. And though I have the gift of prophecy, and understand all mysteries, and all knowledge; and though I have all faith, so that I could remove mountains, and have not charity, I am nothing. And though I bestow all my goods to feed the poor, and though I give my body to be burned, and have not charity, it profiteth me nothing.

1 CORINTHIANS 13:1–3 KJV

"You shall not take vengeance, nor bear any grudge against the sons of your people, but you shall love your neighbor as yourself; I am the LORD."

LEVITICUS 19:18 NASB

Beloved, let us love one another: for love is of God; and every one that loveth is born of God, and knoweth God.

1 JOHN 4:7 KJV

Owe nothing to anyone except to love one another; for he who loves his neighbor has fulfilled the law.

ROMANS 13:8 NASB

"But love your enemies, do good, and lend, hoping for nothing in return; and your reward will be great, and you will be sons of the Most High. For He is kind to the unthankful and evil. Therefore be merciful, just as your Father also is merciful."

LUKE 6:35–36 NKJV

Bear one another's burdens, and thereby fulfill the law of Christ.

GALATIANS 6:2 NASB

"You have heard that it was said, 'You shall love your neighbor and hate your enemy.' But I say to you, love your enemies and pray for those who persecute you, so that you may be sons of your Father who is in heaven; for He causes His sun to rise on the evil and the good, and sends rain on the righteous and the unrighteous."

MATTHEW 5:43–45 NASB

When others are happy, be happy with them. If they are sad, share their sorrow.

ROMANS 12:15 NLT

Now the fruit of righteousness is sown in peace by those who make peace.

JAMES 3:18 NKJV

For this is the message which you have heard from the beginning, that we should love one another.

1 JOHN 3:11 NASB

Be kindly affectioned one to another with brotherly love; in honour preferring one another.

ROMANS 12:10 KJV

"Therefore, if you are offering your gift at the altar and there remember that your brother has something against you, leave your gift there in front of the altar. First go and be reconciled to your brother; then come and offer your gift."

MATTHEW 5:23–24 NIV

Honor all people.
Love the brotherhood.
Fear God.
Honor the king.

1 PETER 2:17 NKJV

So speak and so do as those who will be judged by the law of liberty. For judgment is without mercy to the one who has shown no mercy. Mercy triumphs over judgment.

JAMES 2:12–13 NKJV

Beloved, if God so loved us, we also ought to love one another. No one has seen God at any time. If we love one another, God abides in us, and His love has been perfected in us.

1 JOHN 4:11–12 NKJV

"This is My commandment, that you love one another as I have loved you. Greater love has no one than this, than to lay down one's life for his friends."

JOHN 15:12–13 NKJV

Don't team up with those who are unbelievers. How can goodness be a partner with wickedness? How can light live with darkness?

2 CORINTHIANS 6:14 NLT

Be subject to one another in the fear of Christ.

EPHESIANS 5:21 NASB

Love is patient, love is kind and is not jealous; love does not brag and is not arrogant, does not act unbecomingly; it does not seek its own, is not provoked, does not take into account a wrong suffered.

1 CORINTHIANS 13:4–5 NASB

Thank You, God,

*for the special people in my life,
and for their support, encouragement, and love.
I am so grateful that they accept me as I am—
just as You do.
Please help me to be a good friend, too.
Amen.*

Repentance

Admittedly, it's not fun. Repentance can even be painful—when you recognize that you have sinned against your heavenly Father and need to ask His forgiveness. But as the old workout motto goes, "No pain, no gain." When you do your part by repenting, God does His part by forgiving. He doesn't hold those faults against you, and you've got a clean slate before Him. Easy? No. Worthwhile? Definitely. Is there anything you should repent of today?

Therefore, confess your sins to one another, and pray for one another so that you may be healed. The effective prayer of a righteous man can accomplish much.

JAMES 5:16 NASB

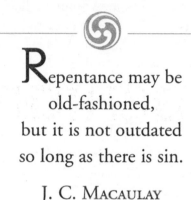

Repentance may be
old-fashioned,
but it is not outdated
so long as there is sin.

J. C. MACAULAY

"But go and learn what this means: 'I desire mercy, not sacrifice.' For I have not come to call the righteous, but sinners."

MATTHEW 9:13 NIV

"If you return to the Almighty, you will be restored; if you remove unrighteousness far from your tent."

JOB 22:23 NASB

Wherefore I say unto you, All manner of sin and blasphemy shall be forgiven unto men: but the blasphemy against the Holy Ghost shall not be forgiven unto men.

MATTHEW 12:31 KJV

The sacrifices of God are a broken spirit, a broken and a contrite heart—these, O God, You will not despise.

PSALM 51:17 NKJV

"But if wicked people turn away from all their sins and begin to obey my laws and do what is just and right, they will surely live and not die. All their past sins will be forgotten, and they will live because of the righteous things they have done. Do you think, asks the Sovereign LORD, that I like to see wicked people die? Of course not! I only want them to turn from their wicked ways and live."

EZEKIEL 18:21–23 NLT

The LORD has heard my supplication; the LORD will receive my prayer.

PSALM 6:9 NKJV

Draw near to God and He will draw near to you. Cleanse your hands, you sinners; and purify your hearts, you double-minded.

JAMES 4:8 NKJV

"God. . .commands all people everywhere to repent."

ACTS 17:30 NIV

Or do you think lightly of the riches of His kindness and tolerance and patience, not knowing that the kindness of God leads you to repentance?

ROMANS 2:4 NASB

The LORD is close to the brokenhearted; he rescues those who are crushed in spirit.

PSALM 34:18 NLT

He who conceals his transgressions will not prosper, but he who confesses and forsakes them will find compassion.

PROVERBS 28:13 NASB

Seek the LORD while He may be found, call upon Him while He is near. Let the wicked forsake his way, and the unrighteous man his thoughts; let him return to the LORD, and He will have mercy on him; and to our God, for He will abundantly pardon.

ISAIAH 55:6–7 NKJV

If we confess our sins, He is faithful and just to forgive us our sins and to cleanse us from all unrighteousness.

1 JOHN 1:9 NKJV

For they themselves report about us what kind of a reception we had with you, and how you turned to God from idols to serve a living and true God, and to wait for His Son from heaven, whom He raised from the dead, that is Jesus, who rescues us from the wrath to come.

1 THESSALONIANS 1:9–10 NASB

"Therefore repent of this wickedness of yours, and pray the Lord that, if possible, the intention of your heart may be forgiven you."

ACTS 8:22 NASB

I acknowledged my sin to You, and my iniquity I have not hidden. I said, "I will confess my transgressions to the LORD," and You forgave the iniquity of my sin.

PSALM 32:5 NKJV

And rend your heart, and not your garments, and turn unto the LORD your God: for he is gracious and merciful, slow to anger, and of great kindness, and repenteth him of the evil.

JOEL 2:13 KJV

"But at last my people will confess their sins and the sins of their ancestors for betraying me and being hostile toward me. Finally, when I have given full expression to my hostility and have brought them to the land of their enemies, then at last their disobedient hearts will be humbled, and they will pay for their sins. Then I will remember my covenant with Jacob, with Isaac, and with Abraham, and I will remember the land."

LEVITICUS 26:40–42 NLT

The time is fulfilled,
and the kingdom of God is at hand;
repent and believe in the gospel."

MARK 1:15 NASB

"Then he will pray to God, and He will accept him, that he may see His face with joy, and He may restore His righteousness to man."

JOB 33:26 NASB

"So remember what you have received and heard; and keep it, and repent. Therefore if you do not wake up, I will come like a thief, and you will not know at what hour I will come to you."

REVELATION 3:3 NASB

Speak unto the children of Israel, When a man or woman shall commit any sin that men commit, to do a trespass against the LORD, and that person be guilty; then they shall confess their sin which they have done: and he shall recompense his trespass with the principal thereof, and add unto it the fifth part thereof, and give it unto him against whom he hath trespassed.

NUMBERS 5:6–7 KJV

Who may ascend into the hill of the LORD? Or who may stand in His holy place? He who has clean hands and a pure heart, who has not lifted up his soul to an idol, nor sworn deceitfully. He shall receive blessing from the LORD, and righteousness from the God of his salvation.

PSALM 24:3–5 NKJV

"Repent, for the kingdom of heaven is at hand!"

MATTHEW 3:2 NKJV

Repent ye therefore, and be converted, that your sins may be blotted out, when the times of refreshing shall come from the presence of the Lord.

ACTS 3:19 KJV

"In the same way, I tell you, there is rejoicing in the presence of the angels of God over one sinner who repents."

LUKE 15:10 NIV

Lord,

I'm sorry for sinning against You.
I know I hurt You when I make the wrong choice.
I commit that with Your help,
I will choose to do what is right no matter what it costs me.
You are much more important to me
than any temptation to sin.
Amen.

Responsibility

I have my rights!" people like to say. What they generally overlook are their *responsibilities*—those duties and obligations of family life, citizenship, or any group membership. For Christians, that responsibility is to conduct their lives in the way that God desires and expects. Responsibility may not always seem like fun, but it is the sign of maturity: There are choices to be made daily that require a spiritual readiness. Live your life prepared to make the right choices, never to be caught offguard by Satan's schemes.

In everything you do, stay away from complaining and arguing, so that no one can speak a word of blame against you. You are to live clean, innocent lives as children of God in a dark world full of crooked and perverse people. Let your lives shine brightly before them. Hold tightly to the word of life, so that when Christ returns, I will be proud that I did not lose the race and that my work was not useless.

PHILIPPIANS 2:14–16 NLT

Y ou cannot escape the
responsibility of tomorrow
by evading it today.

ABRAHAM LINCOLN

And they were both righteous before God, walking in all the commandments and ordinances of the Lord blameless.

LUKE 1:6 NKJV

But let each one examine his own work, and then he will have rejoicing in himself alone, and not in another. For each one shall bear his own load.

GALATIANS 6:4–5 NKJV

"Therefore I will judge you, O house of Israel, each according to his conduct," declares the Lord GOD. "Repent and turn away from all your transgressions, so that iniquity may not become a stumbling block to you."

EZEKIEL 18:30 NASB

Dearly beloved, I beseech you as strangers and pilgrims, abstain from fleshly lusts, which war against the soul; Having your conversation honest among the Gentiles: that, whereas they speak against you as evildoers, they may by your good works, which they shall behold, glorify God in the day of visitation. Submit yourselves to every ordinance of man for the Lord's sake: whether it be to the king, as supreme; Or unto governors, as unto them that are sent by him for the punishment of evildoers, and for the praise of them that do well. For so is the will of God, that with well doing ye may put to silence the ignorance of foolish men: As free, and not using your liberty for a cloke of maliciousness, but as the servants of God.

I PETER 2:11–16 KJV

"I will give to each one of you according to your deeds."

REVELATION 2:23 NASB

Lord Jesus,

help me to make choices that make it clear I'm a Christian.
I'm the only one who can keep my life in check—
not my parents, my pastor, or my friends.
I want to live my life as if there's a spotlight on it
and not hide anything.
That's when I'll have the best relationship
with You and with others.
Amen.

Salvation

Quick—what's the most important thing in your life? Your boyfriend or girlfriend? Your new car? Your family? Your degree? If you're a Christian, the answer should be this: your salvation. God has offered salvation, to all who will accept it, as a free gift. It's free, but not cheap—salvation required the sacrifice of God's only Son, Jesus Christ, on the cross. Why not take a minute to thank God for His gift and for the person who shared the gift of salvation with you? Then go out and share the gift with others.

For by grace you have been saved through faith, and that not of yourselves; it is the gift of God.

EPHESIANS 2:8 NKJV

"Therefore let it be known to you, brethren, that through Him forgiveness of sins is proclaimed to you."

ACTS 13:38 NASB

Each person must decide
for or against Christ.
Turning our backs—
or even just ignoring the question—
results in living in darkness.

JIM GRASSI

My dear children, I am writing this to you so that you will not sin. But if you do sin, there is someone to plead for you before the Father. He is Jesus Christ, the one who pleases God completely. He is the sacrifice for our sins. He takes away not only our sins but the sins of all the world.

1 JOHN 2:1–2 NLT

"He who believes and is baptized will be saved; but he who does not believe will be condemned."

MARK 16:16 NKJV

But to all who believed him and accepted him, he gave the right to become children of God. They are reborn! This is not a physical birth resulting from human passion or plan—this rebirth comes from God.

JOHN 1:12–13 NLT

Jesus answered and said to him, "Truly, truly, I say to you, unless one is born again he cannot see the kingdom of God." Nicodemus said to Him, "How can a man be born when he is old? He cannot enter a second time into his mother's womb and be born, can he?" Jesus answered, "Truly, truly, I say to you, unless one is born of water and the Spirit he cannot enter into the kingdom of God. That which is born of the flesh is flesh, and that which is born of the Spirit is spirit. Do not be amazed that I said to you, 'You must be born again.' "

JOHN 3:3–7 NASB

If you confess with your mouth Jesus as Lord, and believe in your heart that God raised Him from the dead, you will be saved; for with the heart a person believes, resulting in righteousness, and with the mouth he confesses, resulting in salvation. For the Scripture says, "Whoever believes in Him will not be disappointed." For there is no distinction between Jew and Greek; for the same Lord is Lord of all, abounding in riches for all who call on Him; for "Whoever will call on the name of the Lord will be saved."

ROMANS 10:9–13 NASB

"Look! Here I stand at the door and knock. If you hear me calling and open the door, I will come in, and we will share a meal as friends."

REVELATION 3:20 NLT

For this is good and acceptable in the sight of God our Savior, who desires all men to be saved and to come to the knowledge of the truth.

1 TIMOTHY 2:3–4 NKJV

"I am the door; if anyone enters through Me, he will be saved, and will go in and out and find pasture."

JOHN 10:9 NASB

"He who believes in Him is not condemned; but he who does not believe is condemned already, because he has not believed in the name of the only begotten Son of God."

JOHN 3:18 NKJV

God made him who had no sin to be sin for us, so that in him we might become the righteousness of God.

2 CORINTHIANS 5:21 NIV

"I tell you that in the same way, there will be more joy in heaven over one sinner who repents than over ninety-nine righteous persons who need no repentance."

LUKE 15:7 NASB

"I give eternal life to them, and they will never perish; and no one will snatch them out of My hand."

JOHN 10:28 NASB

"Nor is there salvation in any other, for there is no other name under heaven given among men by which we must be saved."

ACTS 4:12 NKJV

But when the kindness and the love of God our Savior toward man appeared, not by works of righteousness which we have done, but according to His mercy He saved us, through the washing of regeneration and renewing of the Holy Spirit, whom He poured out on us abundantly through Jesus Christ our Savior.

TITUS 3:4–6 NKJV

And they said,
Believe on the Lord Jesus Christ,
and thou shalt be saved,
and thy house.

ACTS 16:31 KJV

"Enter through the narrow gate. For wide is the gate and broad is the road that leads to destruction, and many enter through it. But small is the gate and narrow the road that leads to life, and only a few find it."

MATTHEW 7:13–14 NIV

"He who believes in the Son has eternal life; but he who does not obey the Son will not see life, but the wrath of God abides on him."

JOHN 3:36 NASB

Therefore, if anyone is in Christ, he is a new creation; old things have passed away; behold, all things have become new.

2 CORINTHIANS 5:17 NKJV

Therefore lay aside all filthiness and overflow of wickedness, and receive with meekness the implanted word, which is able to save your souls.

JAMES 1:21 NKJV

Thank You, God,

for sending Your Son to die for me.
I know I deserved that terrible death sentence,
but You spared me because of Your love for me.
You made a huge sacrifice,
and I was given the free gift of salvation.
Thank You!
Amen.

Scripture

Ever wish that life had an owner's manual, like your car or your computer do? Well, life does—it's called the Bible. God's Word is the Christian's manual for a happy and productive life—but only if it's used properly. Take the Bible off your shelf and read it every day. Memorize important scriptures and bring them to mind when trouble or temptation strikes. God's Word can bring comfort and strength when you need them most.

Let the word of Christ richly dwell within you, with all wisdom teaching and admonishing one another with psalms and hymns and spiritual songs, singing with thankfulness in your hearts to God.

COLOSSIANS 3:16 NASB

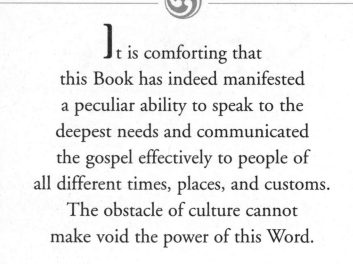

It is comforting that
this Book has indeed manifested
a peculiar ability to speak to the
deepest needs and communicated
the gospel effectively to people of
all different times, places, and customs.
The obstacle of culture cannot
make void the power of this Word.

R. C. SPROUL

I have hidden your word in my heart, that I might not sin against you.

PSALM 119:11 NLT

"As for God, His way is blameless; the word of the LORD is tested; He is a shield to all who take refuge in Him."

2 SAMUEL 22:31 NASB

But you must continue in the things which you have learned and been assured of, knowing from whom you have learned them, and that from childhood you have known the Holy Scriptures, which are able to make you wise for salvation through faith which is in Christ Jesus.

2 TIMOTHY 3:14–15 NKJV

You should remember the words spoken beforehand by the holy prophets and the commandment of the Lord and Savior spoken by your apostles.

2 PETER 3:2 NASB

So shall my word be that goeth forth out of my mouth: it shall not return unto me void, but it shall accomplish that which I please, and it shall prosper in the thing whereto I sent it.

ISAIAH 55:11 KJV

Your word is a lamp to my feet and a light for my path.

PSALM 119:105 NIV

For the word of God is living and powerful, and sharper than any two-edged sword, piercing even to the division of soul and spirit, and of joints and marrow, and is a discerner of the thoughts and intents of the heart.

HEBREWS 4:12 NKJV

My son, give attention to my words; incline your ear to my sayings. Do not let them depart from your eyes; keep them in the midst of your heart; for they are life to those who find them, and health to all their flesh.

PROVERBS 4:20–22 NKJV

The statutes of the LORD are right, rejoicing the heart; the commandment of the LORD is pure, enlightening the eyes.

PSALM 19:8 NKJV

Forever, O LORD, Your word is settled in heaven.

PSALM 119:89 NKJV

"So commit yourselves completely to these words of mine. Tie them to your hands as a reminder, and wear them on your forehead. Teach them to your children. Talk about them when you are at home and when you are away on a journey, when you are lying down and when you are getting up again."

DEUTERONOMY 11:18–19 NLT

Seek ye out of the book of the LORD, and read: no one of these shall fail, none shall want her mate: for my mouth it hath commanded, and his spirit it hath gathered them.

ISAIAH 34:16 KJV

All Scripture is inspired by God and profitable for teaching, for reproof, for correction, for training in righteousness; so that the man of God may be adequate, equipped for every good work.

2 TIMOTHY 3:16–17 NASB

But know this first of all, that no prophecy of Scripture is a matter of one's own interpretation, for no prophecy was ever made by an act of human will, but men moved by the Holy Spirit spoke from God.

2 PETER 1:20–21 NASB

"Do not let this Book of the Law depart from your mouth; meditate on it day and night, so that you may be careful to do everything written in it. Then you will be prosperous and successful."

JOSHUA 1:8 NIV

Heavenly Father,

thank You for giving us Your Word.
Please help me to take the time to
read it and meditate on it.
I'm sorry for the days that
I get so busy I rush past my Bible without opening it.
I want to spend time listening to the things
that You have to say to me.
Amen.

Self-Control

Get a grip, will ya? Or in other words, keep control over yourself—Christians and non-Christians alike are watching to see how you react to the situations of life. Your choice to stand strong in your faith, to resist temptation, or to respond in love will be an encouragement to others. However, a thoughtless word or action can destroy the testimony you're trying to maintain. Who do you really want to be? Much of the answer to that question comes down to self-control.

Or do you not know that the unrighteous will not inherit the kingdom of God? Do not be deceived; neither fornicators, nor idolaters, nor adulterers, nor effeminate, nor homosexuals, nor thieves, nor the covetous, nor drunkards, nor revilers, nor swindlers, will inherit the kingdom of God. Such were some of you; but you were washed, but you were sanctified, but you were justified in the name of the Lord Jesus Christ and in the Spirit of our God.

1 CORINTHIANS 6:9-11 NASB

Moral failure is rarely
the result of a blowout;
almost always, it's the result of a slow leak.

GARY OLIVER

For the grace of God that bringeth salvation hath appeared to all men, teaching us that, denying ungodliness and worldly lusts, we should live soberly, righteously, and godly, in this present world; looking for that blessed hope, and the glorious appearing of the great God and our Saviour Jesus Christ; who gave himself for us, that he might redeem us from all iniquity, and purify unto himself a peculiar people, zealous of good works.

TITUS 2:11–14 KJV

For you have been called for this purpose, since Christ also suffered for you, leaving you an example for you to follow in His steps, who committed no sin, nor was any deceit found in His mouth; and while being reviled, He did not revile in return; while suffering, He uttered no threats, but kept entrusting Himself to Him who judges righteously.

1 PETER 2:21–23 NASB

Whoever has no rule over his own spirit is like a city broken down, without walls.

PROVERBS 25:28 NKJV

But also for this very reason, giving all diligence, add to your faith virtue, to virtue knowledge, to knowledge self-control, to self-control perseverance, to perseverance godliness, to godliness brotherly kindness, and to brotherly kindness love. For if these things are yours and abound, you will be neither barren nor unfruitful in the knowledge of our Lord Jesus Christ.

2 PETER 1:5–8 NKJV

So, dear brothers and sisters, you have no obligation whatsoever to do what your sinful nature urges you to do. For if you keep on following it, you will perish. But if through the power of the Holy Spirit you turn from it and its evil deeds, you will live.

ROMANS 8:12–13 NLT

Let your gentleness be known to all men. The Lord is at hand.

PHILIPPIANS 4:5 NKJV

Lord,

*I like to have fun and hang out with my friends.
Help me to refuse to go along with them
when they do things that aren't pleasing to You.
I want my words and actions to be those
that make it obvious I'm a Christian.*

Amen.

Sin

Such a little word. . .such big consequences. Sin is any thought or action that goes against God's will—like that dreaded "fruit incident" in the Garden of Eden that's plagued humanity ever since. Because our human nature, we will all sin. That, however, is not a license to sin. While God knows we will sin, He has also provided a way of escape so that we can avoid sin's consequences and live to please Him. That way of escape is Jesus.

My dear children, I write this to you so that you will not sin. But if anybody does sin, we have one who speaks to the Father in our defense—Jesus Christ, the Righteous One. He is the atoning sacrifice for our sins, and not only for ours but also for the sins of the whole world.

1 JOHN 2:1-2 NIV

Christ's death and resurrection marked the end of sin's power to control the believer. Just as sin could not control the Son of God, so it is powerless to control those who have been placed into Christ through faith.

CHARLES STANLEY

This is a faithful saying and worthy of all acceptance, that Christ Jesus came into the world to save sinners, of whom I am chief.

1 TIMOTHY 1:15 NKJV

Our old self was crucified with Him, in order that our body of sin might be done away with, so that we would no longer be slaves to sin; for he who has died is freed from sin.

ROMANS 6:6–7 NASB

He has removed our rebellious acts as far away from us as the east is from the west.

PSALM 103:12 NLT

Grace and peace to you from God our Father and the Lord Jesus Christ, who gave himself for our sins to rescue us from the present evil age, according to the will of our God and Father.

GALATIANS 1:3–4 NIV

Who Himself bore our sins in His own body on the tree, that we, having died to sins, might live for righteousness—by whose stripes you were healed.

1 PETER 2:24 NKJV

"Of Him all the prophets bear witness that through His name everyone who believes in Him receives forgiveness of sins."

ACTS 10:43 NASB

Your eyes are too pure to approve evil, and You can not look on wickedness with favor. Why do You look with favor on those who deal treacherously? Why are You silent when the wicked swallow up those more righteous than they?

HABAKKUK 1:13 NASB

But he was wounded for our transgressions, he was bruised for our iniquities: the chastisement of our peace was upon him; and with his stripes we are healed. All we like sheep have gone astray; we have turned every one to his own way; and the LORD hath laid on him the iniquity of us all.

ISAIAH 53:5–6 KJV

"For I will be merciful to their unrighteousness, and their sins and their lawless deeds I will remember no more."

HEBREWS 8:12 NKJV

God's law was given so that all people could see how sinful they were. But as people sinned more and more, God's wonderful kindness became more abundant.

ROMANS 5:20 NLT

If we walk in the Light as He Himself is in the Light, we have fellowship with one another, and the blood of Jesus His Son cleanses us from all sin.

1 JOHN 1:7 NASB

"Come now, and let us reason together," says the LORD, "though your sins are like scarlet, they shall be as white as snow; though they are red like crimson, they shall be as wool."

ISAIAH 1:18 NKJV

Heavenly Father,

I'm so sorry for the sins that I've committed, even today.
I want to repent of them now,
promising to leave them in the past.
Nothing is worth separating me from You.
I pray with Your help that
I'll defeat Satan's attempts to keep me from
living the life You want for me.
Amen.

Sobriety

*S*obriety is one of those words you don't hear used a lot these days. But the concept is timeless—it's all about keeping your mind under your own control, and not relinquishing that control to alcohol, drugs, or anything else. If your mind is controlled by anything other than the Holy Spirit, there may be some disastrous consequences. Sobriety is essential in the Christian life.

Wine is a mocker, strong drink a brawler, and whoever is intoxicated by it is not wise.

PROVERBS 20:1 NASB

Do not be with heavy drinkers of wine, or with gluttonous eaters of meat. . . . Do not look on the wine when it is red, when it sparkles in the cup, when it goes down smoothly; at the last it bites like a serpent and stings like a viper.

PROVERBS 23:20, 31–32 NASB

T he hard part about
being a bartender is figuring out
who is drunk and who is just stupid.

RICHARD BRAUNSTEIN

Woe unto them that are mighty to drink wine, and men of strength to mingle strong drink.

ISAIAH 5:22 KJV

So whether you eat or drink or whatever you do, do it all for the glory of God.

1 CORINTHIANS 10:31 NIV

"Now therefore, be careful not to drink wine or strong drink, nor eat any unclean thing."

JUDGES 13:4 NASB

They will eat, but not have enough; they will play the harlot, but not increase, because they have stopped giving heed to the LORD. Harlotry, wine and new wine take away the understanding.

HOSEA 4:10–11 NASB

Like tangled thorns, and like those who are drunken with their drink, they are consumed as stubble completely withered.

NAHUM 1:10 NASB

Be sober, be vigilant; because your adversary the devil walks about like a roaring lion, seeking whom he may devour.

1 PETER 5:8 NKJV

Let us walk properly, as in the day, not in revelry and drunkenness, not in lewdness and lust, not in strife and envy.

ROMANS 13:13 NKJV

"How terrible it will be for you who make your neighbors drunk! You force your cup on them so that you can gloat over their nakedness and shame."

HABAKKUK 2:15 NLT

Therefore let us not sleep, as others do, but let us watch and be sober. For those who sleep, sleep at night, and those who get drunk are drunk at night.

1 THESSALONIANS 5:6–7 NKJV

"But take heed to yourselves, lest your hearts be weighed down with carousing, drunkenness, and cares of this life, and that Day come on you unexpectedly."

LUKE 21:34 NKJV

The acts of the sinful nature are obvious: sexual immorality, impurity and debauchery; idolatry and witchcraft; hatred, discord, jealousy, fits of rage, selfish ambition, dissensions, factions and envy; drunkenness, orgies, and the like. I warn you, as I did before, that those who live like this will not inherit the kingdom of God.

GALATIANS 5:19–21 NIV

For the grace of God that brings salvation has appeared to all men, teaching us that, denying ungodliness and worldly lusts, we should live soberly, righteously, and godly in the present age, looking for the blessed hope and glorious appearing of our great God and Savior Jesus Christ.

TITUS 2:11–13 NKJV

For the heavy drinker and the glutton will come to poverty, and drowsiness will clothe one with rags.

PROVERBS 23:21 NASB

Don't be drunk with wine, because that will ruin your life. Instead, let the Holy Spirit fill and control you. Then you will sing psalms and hymns and spiritual songs among yourselves, making music to the Lord in your hearts. And you will always give thanks for everything to God the Father in the name of our Lord Jesus Christ.

EPHESIANS 5:18–20 NLT

Woe to those who rise early in the morning, that they may follow intoxicating drink; who continue until night, till wine inflames them!

ISAIAH 5:11 NKJV

Who has woe? Who has sorrow? Who has contentions? Who has complaining? Who has wounds without cause? Who has redness of eyes? Those who linger long over wine, those who go to taste mixed wine.

PROVERBS 23:29–30 NASB

It is good neither to eat flesh, nor to drink wine, nor any thing whereby thy brother stumbleth, or is offended, or is made weak.

ROMANS 14:21 KJV

You are all sons of light and sons of day. We are not of night nor of darkness; so then let us not sleep as others do, but let us be alert and sober.

1 THESSALONIANS 5:5–6 NASB

Do you not know that you are the temple of God and that the Spirit of God dwells in you? If anyone defiles the temple of God, God will destroy him. For the temple of God is holy, which temple you are.

1 CORINTHIANS 3:16–17 NKJV

Dear God,

I want to keep my mind clear and focused on You.
Give me the strength to say "no" when
I am tempted to use any substance that
might cause me harm.
You have given me the freedom to choose,
and I choose You.
Amen.

Temptation

Have you seen the bumper sticker that says, I CAN RESIST ANYTHING BUT TEMPTATION? It's funny, but it's also pretty accurate. Temptation is strong stuff—why else do you think Satan would use it so much? When you face temptation, remember that Christ Himself was also tempted. If Jesus could be tempted, it stands to reason that there is no sin in being tempted; you sin when you give in to temptation. Jesus fought off Satan's temptations by quoting scripture and remaining faithful to His heavenly Father—just as we should do.

For we do not have a high priest who cannot sympathize with our weaknesses, but One who has been tempted in all things as we are, yet without sin. Therefore let us draw near with confidence to the throne of grace, so that we may receive mercy and find grace to help in time of need.

HEBREWS 4:15–16 NASB

While external circumstances
often contribute to our sinning,
temptation begins in the heart.
Our minds and hearts choose to
sin long before we commit the act.

WARREN WIERSBE

When He came to the place, He said to them, "Pray that you may not enter into temptation."

LUKE 22:40 NKJV

Though he fall, he shall not be utterly cast down: for the LORD upholdeth him with his hand.

PSALM 37:24 KJV

Great peace have those who love Your law, and nothing causes them to stumble.

PSALM 119:165 NKJV

"Watch and pray so that you will not fall into temptation. The spirit is willing, but the body is weak."

MATTHEW 26:41 NIV

Blessed is a man who perseveres under trial; for once he has been approved, he will receive the crown of life which the Lord has promised to those who love Him. Let no one say when he is tempted, "I am being tempted by God"; for God cannot be tempted by evil, and He Himself does not tempt anyone. But each one is tempted when he is carried away and enticed by his own lust. Then when lust has conceived, it gives birth to sin; and when sin is accomplished, it brings forth death.

JAMES 1:12–15 NASB

Therefore let him who thinks he stands take heed that he does not fall. No temptation has overtaken you but such as is common to man; and God is faithful, who will not allow you to be tempted beyond what you are able, but with the temptation will provide the way of escape also, so that you will be able to endure it.

1 CORINTHIANS 10:12–13 NASB

So you see, the Lord knows how to rescue godly people from their trials, even while punishing the wicked right up until the day of judgment.

2 PETER 2:9 NLT

"And do not lead us into temptation, but deliver us from evil. [For Yours is the kingdom and the power and the glory forever. Amen.]"

MATTHEW 6:13 NASB

Lord,

*I need Your strength
when I'm tempted to do the wrong thing.
Each day holds so many choices,
and I want to make the right ones.
Please help me to stand strong so that
those who are watching me can see
the benefit of choosing to do right.
Amen.*

Thought Life

Your thought life is the most private part of you—who are you, really? It is possible to hide those innermost thoughts from others, but God sees all of them, good or bad. If you struggle with impure thoughts, God is able to clean your mind. Confess your sins and replace those bad thoughts with God's Word. It may take time and effort, but you'll find it's well worth the investment.

Do not conform any longer to the pattern of this world, but be transformed by the renewing of your mind. Then you will be able to test and approve what God's will is—his good, pleasing and perfect will.

ROMANS 12:2 NIV

A man's what
he thinks about all day long.

RALPH WALDO EMERSON

I remember the days of old; I meditate on all Your works; I muse on the work of Your hands.

PSALM 143:5 NKJV

Evil plans are an abomination to the LORD, but pleasant words are pure.

PROVERBS 15:26 NASB

For "who has known the mind of the LORD that he may instruct Him?" But we have the mind of Christ.

1 CORINTHIANS 2:16 NKJV

And He said to him, " 'You shall love the Lord your God with all your heart, and with all your soul, and with all your mind.' "

MATTHEW 22:37 NASB

Since you have been raised to new life with Christ, set your sights on the realities of heaven, where Christ sits at God's right hand in the place of honor and power. Let heaven fill your thoughts. Do not think only about things down here on earth. For you died when Christ died, and your real life is hidden with Christ in God. And when Christ, who is your real life, is revealed to the whole world, you will share in all his glory.

COLOSSIANS 3:1–4 NLT

Keep your heart with all diligence, for out of it spring the issues of life.

PROVERBS 4:23 NKJV

Search me, O God, and know my heart: try me, and know my thoughts: And see if there be any wicked way in me, and lead me in the way everlasting.

PSALM 139:23–24 KJV

"You will keep him in perfect peace, whose mind is stayed on You, because he trusts in You."

ISAIAH 26:3 NKJV

"The good man brings good things out of the good stored up in his heart, and the evil man brings evil things out of the evil stored up in his heart. For out of the overflow of his heart his mouth speaks."

LUKE 6:45 NIV

For the word of God is full of living power. It is sharper than the sharpest knife, cutting deep into our innermost thoughts and desires. It exposes us for what we really are.

HEBREWS 4:12 NLT

Let the words of my mouth and the meditation of my heart be acceptable in Your sight, O LORD, my strength and my Redeemer.

PSALM 19:14 NKJV

"As for you, my son Solomon, know the God of your father, and serve Him with a whole heart and a willing mind; for the LORD searches all hearts, and understands every intent of the thoughts. If you seek Him, He will let you find Him; but if you forsake Him, He will reject you forever."

1 CHRONICLES 28:9 NASB

Let the wicked forsake his way and the evil man his thoughts. Let him turn to the LORD, and he will have mercy on him, and to our God, for he will freely pardon.

ISAIAH 55:7 NIV

Examine me, O LORD, and prove me; try my mind and my heart. For Your lovingkindness is before my eyes, and I have walked in Your truth.

PSALM 26:2–3 NKJV

"I, the LORD, search the heart, I test the mind, even to give to each man according to his ways, according to the results of his deeds."

JEREMIAH 17:10 NASB

For from within, out of the heart of men, proceed evil thoughts, adulteries, fornications, murders, thefts, covetousness, wickedness, deceit, lasciviousness, an evil eye, blasphemy, pride, foolishness: All these evil things come from within, and defile the man.

MARK 7:21–23 KJV

Create in me a clean heart, O God, and renew a steadfast spirit within me.

PSALM 51:10 NASB

For those who are according to the flesh set their minds on the things of the flesh, but those who are according to the Spirit, the things of the Spirit. For the mind set on the flesh is death, but the mind set on the Spirit is life and peace.

ROMANS 8:5–6 NASB

Bringing every thought into captivity to the obedience of Christ.

2 CORINTHIANS 10:5 NKJV

When I was a child, I spoke as a child, I understood as a child, I thought as a child; but when I became a man, I put away childish things.

1 CORINTHIANS 13:11 NKJV

I will meditate on all Your work and muse on Your deeds.

PSALM 77:12 NASB

The peace of God, which surpasses all understanding, will guard your hearts and minds through Christ Jesus.

PHILIPPIANS 4:7 NKJV

"But seek first His kingdom and His righteousness, and all these things will be added to you."

MATTHEW 6:33 NASB

Thou knowest my downsitting and mine uprising, thou understandest my thought afar off.

PSALM 139:2 KJV

Throw off your old evil nature and your former way of life, which is rotten through and through, full of lust and deception. Instead, there must be a spiritual renewal of your thoughts and attitudes.

EPHESIANS 4:22–23 NLT

Finally, brothers, whatever is true, whatever is noble, whatever is right, whatever is pure, whatever is lovely, whatever is admirable—if anything is excellent or praiseworthy—think about such things.

PHILIPPIANS 4:8 NIV

Lord Jesus,

I give my thought life to You.
Please fill my mind with pure thoughts—
ones that will please You.
Forgive me for any sinful thoughts I've had today
and help me to renew my mind.
Amen.

Unity

Christians of the world, unite! God wants His people, regardless of race, denomination, or social status, to be unified in the purpose of serving Him and fulfilling the Great Commission. Don't allow barriers to separate you from your fellow Christians—you'll be worshipping the Lord with them in heaven someday.

Now I plead with you, brethren, by the name of our Lord Jesus Christ, that you all speak the same thing, and that there be no divisions among you, but that you be perfectly joined together in the same mind and in the same judgment.

1 CORINTHIANS 1:10 NKJV

B ecause God reconciled us
to Himself through His only Son, Jesus Christ,
we are going to reconcile with
our Christian brothers of different
races, cultures, and denominations.

BILL MCCARTNEY

Always keep yourselves united in the Holy Spirit, and bind yourselves together with peace.

EPHESIANS 4:3 NLT

Do two walk together unless they have agreed to do so?

AMOS 3:3 NIV

Behold, how good and how pleasant it is for brethren to dwell together in unity!

PSALM 133:1 NKJV

Their hearts may be encouraged, having been knit to-gether in love, and attaining to all the wealth that comes from the full assurance of understanding, resulting in a true knowledge of God's mystery, that is, Christ Himself, in whom are hidden all the treasures of wisdom and knowledge.

COLOSSIANS 2:2–3 NASB

Be of the same mind toward one another; do not be haughty in mind, but associate with the lowly. Do not be wise in your own estimation.

ROMANS 12:16 NASB

And He Himself gave some to be apostles, some prophets, some evangelists, and some pastors and teachers, for the equipping of the saints for the work of ministry, for the edifying of the body of Christ, till we all come to the unity of the faith and of the knowledge of the Son of God, to a perfect man, to the measure of the stature of the fullness of Christ.

EPHESIANS 4:11–13 NKJV

Now may the God who gives perseverance and encourage-ment grant you to be of the same mind with one another according to Christ Jesus, so that with one accord you may with one voice glorify the God and Father of our Lord Jesus Christ.

ROMANS 15:5–6 NASB

For we were all baptized by one Spirit into one body—whether Jews or Greeks, slave or free—and we were all given the one Spirit to drink.

1 CORINTHIANS 12:13 NIV

Beyond all these things put on love, which is the perfect bond of unity.

COLOSSIANS 3:14 NASB

Therefore if there is any consolation in Christ, if any comfort of love, if any fellowship of the Spirit, if any affection and mercy, fulfill my joy by being like-minded, having the same love, being of one accord, of one mind.

PHILIPPIANS 2:1–2 NKJV

Father,

help me not to judge others because they're different.
You have created them, and we're equal in Your eyes.
I want to be willing to share Your love with
everyone I come in contact with,
regardless of our differences.
Give me the ability to love others
the way that You love them.
Amen.

Wisdom

Know somebody who's smart? Know anybody who's wise? There is a difference. God wants us to be wise—people who properly use their knowledge. The catch is that we can't be wise in our own power. So, as usual, God will provide what we need. The wisdom He expects us to show is free for the asking (James 1:5).

If any of you lacks wisdom, let him ask of God, who gives to all liberally and without reproach, and it will be given to him. But let him ask in faith, with no doubting, for he who doubts is like a wave of the sea driven and tossed by the wind. For let not that man suppose that he will receive anything from the Lord; he is a double-minded man, unstable in all his ways.

JAMES 1:5–8 NKJV

How much better is it to get wisdom than gold! and to get understanding rather to be chosen than silver!

PROVERBS 16:16 KJV

A wise son maketh a glad father: but a foolish son is the heaviness of his mother.

PROVERBS 10:1 KJV

Wisdom and knowledge will be the stability of your times, and the strength of salvation; the fear of the LORD is His treasure.

ISAIAH 33:6 NKJV

Whoever gives heed to instruction prospers, and blessed is he who trusts in the LORD. The wise in heart are called discerning, and pleasant words promote instruction.

PROVERBS 16:20–21 NIV

Who is wise? Let him give heed to these things, and consider the lovingkindnesses of the LORD.

PSALM 107:43 NASB

For the report of your obedience has reached to all; therefore I am rejoicing over you, but I want you to be wise in what is good and innocent in what is evil.

ROMANS 16:19 NASB

W isdom is the
right use of knowledge.
To know is not to be wise.
Many men know a great deal
and are all the greater fools for it.
There is no fool so great a fool as a knowing fool.
But to know how to use knowledge
is to have wisdom.

CHARLES SPURGEON

Those who are wise shall shine like the brightness of the firmament, and those who turn many to righteousness like the stars forever and ever.

DANIEL 12:3 NKJV

Let those who are wise understand these things. Let those who are discerning listen carefully. The paths of the LORD are true and right, and righteous people live by walking in them. But sinners stumble and fall along the way.

HOSEA 14:9 NLT

Love wisdom like a sister; make insight a beloved member of your family.

PROVERBS 7:4 NLT

The teaching of the wise is a fountain of life, to turn aside from the snares of death. Good understanding produces favor, but the way of the treacherous is hard.

PROVERBS 13:14–15 NASB

"Get wisdom! Get understanding! Do not forget, nor turn away from the words of my mouth. Do not forsake her, and she will preserve you; love her, and she will keep you. Wisdom is the principal thing; therefore get wisdom. And in all your getting, get understanding. Exalt her, and she will promote you; she will bring you honor, when you embrace her. She will place on your head an ornament of grace; a crown of glory she will deliver to you." Hear, my son, and receive my sayings, and the years of your life will be many. I have taught you in the way of wisdom; I have led you in right paths. When you walk, your steps will not be hindered, and when you run, you will not stumble. Take firm hold of instruction, do not let go; keep her, for she is your life.

PROVERBS 4:5–13 NKJV

"Therefore everyone who hears these words of Mine and acts on them, may be compared to a wise man who built his house on the rock. And the rain fell, and the floods came, and the winds blew and slammed against that house; and yet it did not fall, for it had been founded on the rock."

MATTHEW 7:24–25 NASB

"I, wisdom, dwell together with prudence; I possess knowledge and discretion."

PROVERBS 8:12 NIV

But if any of you lacks wisdom,
let him ask of God,
who gives to all generously
and without reproach,
and it will be given to him.

JAMES 1:5 NASB

He who keeps his command will experience nothing harmful; and a wise man's heart discerns both time and judgment.

ECCLESIASTES 8:5 NKJV

However, we speak wisdom among those who are mature, yet not the wisdom of this age, nor of the rulers of this age, who are coming to nothing. But we speak the wisdom of God in a mystery, the hidden wisdom which God ordained before the ages for our glory, which none of the rulers of this age knew; for had they known, they would not have crucified the Lord of glory.

1 CORINTHIANS 2:6–8 NKJV

Who is a wise man and endued with knowledge among you? let him shew out of a good conversation his works with meekness of wisdom. But if ye have bitter envying and strife in your hearts, glory not, and lie not against the truth. This wisdom descendeth not from above, but is earthly, sensual, devilish. . . . But the wisdom that is from above is first pure, then peaceable, gentle, and easy to be intreated, full of mercy and good fruits, without partiality, and without hypocrisy.

JAMES 3:13–15, 17 KJV

Dear Lord,

I thank You for the mind You have given me.
Please give me the good judgment I need
in the choices that I face every day.
You promised Solomon anything he asked for,
and he chose wisdom.
I'm grateful that You will give me wisdom, too,
if I'll only ask for it.
Amen.

Witnessing

Look in the dictionary, and you'll find that the word *witness* can mean "one who has personal knowledge of something." If you're a Christian, you qualify as a witness—someone who knows Jesus Christ and can tell others about Him. We cross paths with non-Christians every day—and you may be the only Christian that a lost person meets. Be a shining example of Christ in both your words and actions. Because of your testimony, someone may have the privilege of being saved just like you were.

Yet for this reason I found mercy, so that in me as the fore-most, Jesus Christ might demonstrate His perfect patience as an example for those who would believe in Him for eternal life.

1 TIMOTHY 1:16 NASB

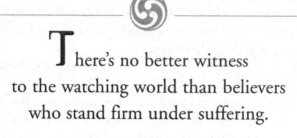

There's no better witness
to the watching world than believers
who stand firm under suffering.

MICHAEL W. SMITH

"You are the light of the world. A city on a hill cannot be hidden. Neither do people light a lamp and put it under a bowl. Instead they put it on its stand, and it gives light to everyone in the house. In the same way, let your light shine before men, that they may see your good deeds and praise your Father in heaven."

MATTHEW 5:14–16 NIV

And have no fellowship with the unfruitful works of darkness, but rather expose them. For it is shameful even to speak of those things which are done by them in secret. But all things that are exposed are made manifest by the light, for whatever makes manifest is light.

EPHESIANS 5:11–13 NKJV

Therefore do not be ashamed of the testimony of our Lord, nor of me His prisoner, but share with me in the sufferings for the gospel according to the power of God.

2 TIMOTHY 1:8 NKJV

My brethren, if any among you strays from the truth and one turns him back, let him know that he who turns a sinner from the error of his way will save his soul from death and will cover a multitude of sins.

JAMES 5:19–20 NASB

Rescuing you from the Jewish people and from the Gentiles, to whom I am sending you, to open their eyes so that they may turn from darkness to light and from the dominion of Satan to God, that they may receive forgiveness of sins and an inheritance among those who have been sanctified by faith in Me.

ACTS 26:17–18 NASB

Preach the word! Be ready in season and out of season. Convince, rebuke, exhort, with all longsuffering and teaching.

2 TIMOTHY 4:2 NKJV

But in your hearts set apart Christ as Lord. Always be prepared to give an answer to everyone who asks you to give the reason for the hope that you have. But do this with gentleness and respect.

1 PETER 3:15 NIV

Let the redeemed of the LORD say so, whom He has redeemed from the hand of the adversary.

PSALM 107:2 NASB

Dear God,

*give me the words to say when I tell others about You
and what You've done in my life.
Please help me to always be ready to talk about You.
And help me to remember that others will be
watching my life to see if what I say matches what I do.
Amen.*

Worship

Worship isn't only for church. At work, in the car, exercising, whenever—we can be in a constant state of worship, praising God for His goodness. He doesn't expect eloquent or lengthy prayers. (In fact, God is probably most pleased with the simplest words—that child-like faith, you know.) Wherever you are, whatever you're doing, just express to God your thankfulness for Him.

Come, let us worship and bow down. Let us kneel before the LORD our maker.

PSALM 95:6 NLT

"But an hour is coming, and now is, when the true worshipers will worship the Father in spirit and truth; for such people the Father seeks to be His worshipers. God is spirit, and those who worship Him must worship in spirit and truth."

JOHN 4:23–24 NASB

W hen we're alone with God,
there are no more distractions
to the development of intimacy.
It is just us and Him.
The rest of the world must wait.

WELLINGTON BOONE

"Then the sovereignty, the dominion and the greatness of all the kingdoms under the whole heaven will be given to the people of the saints of the Highest One; His kingdom will be an everlasting kingdom, and all the dominions will serve and obey Him."

DANIEL 7:27 NASB

Then I saw another angel flying in the midst of heaven, having the everlasting gospel to preach to those who dwell on the earth—to every nation, tribe, tongue, and people—saying with a loud voice, "Fear God and give glory to Him, for the hour of His judgment has come; and worship Him who made heaven and earth, the sea and springs of water."

REVELATION 14:6–7 NKJV

"You alone are the LORD. You have made the heavens, the heaven of heavens with all their host, the earth and all that is on it, the seas and all that is in them. You give life to all of them and the heavenly host bows down before You."

NEHEMIAH 9:6 NASB

And Jesus answered and said to him, "Get behind Me, Satan! For it is written, 'You shall worship the LORD your God, and Him only you shall serve.' "

LUKE 4:8 NKJV

"Do not follow other gods to serve and worship them; do not provoke me to anger with what your hands have made. Then I will not harm you."

JEREMIAH 25:6 NIV

"Who shall not fear You, O Lord, and glorify Your name? For You alone are holy. For all nations shall come and worship before You, for Your judgments have been manifested."

REVELATION 15:4 NKJV

Therefore, since we receive a kingdom which cannot be shaken, let us show gratitude, by which we may offer to God an acceptable service with reverence and awe.

HEBREWS 12:28 NASB

All the nations—and you made each one—will come and bow before you, Lord; they will praise your great and holy name.

PSALM 86:9 NLT

"But the LORD your God you shall fear; and He will deliver you from the hand of all your enemies."

2 KINGS 17:39 NKJV

Ascribe to the LORD the glory due His name; bring an offering, and come before Him; worship the LORD in holy array.

1 CHRONICLES 16:29 NASB

I beseech you therefore, brethren, by the mercies of God, that ye present your bodies a living sacrifice, holy, acceptable unto God, which is your reasonable service.

ROMANS 12:1 KJV

Serve the LORD with gladness: come before his presence with singing.

PSALM 100:2 KJV

Father,

You are holy, and Lord over all.
At times, I feel so small when I think of Your greatness.
I'm amazed that You take the time to listen to me.
You make me feel important and so loved, and I thank You.
I praise You for all that You have done in my life.
Amen.

Schedule for Reading Through the Bible in a Year

Bible Readings for January

January 1 - LUKE 5:27–39, GENESIS 1–2, PSALM 1
January 2 - LUKE 6:1–26, GENESIS 3–5, PSALM 2
January 3 - LUKE 6:27–49, GENESIS 6–7, PSALM 3
January 4 - LUKE 7:1–17, GENESIS 8–10, PSALM 4
January 5 - LUKE 7:18–50, GENESIS 11, PSALM 5
January 6 - LUKE 8:1–25, GENESIS 12, PSALM 6
January 7 - LUKE 8:26–56, GENESIS 13–14, PSALM 7
January 8 - LUKE 9:1–27, GENESIS 15, PSALM 8
January 9 - LUKE 9:28–62, GENESIS 16, PSALM 9
January 10 - LUKE 10:1–20, GENESIS 17, PSALM 10
January 11 - LUKE 10:21–42, GENESIS 18, PSALM 11
January 12 - LUKE 11:1–28, GENESIS 19, PSALM 12
January 13 - LUKE 11:29–54, GENESIS 20, PSALM 13
January 14 - LUKE 12:1–31, GENESIS 21, PSALM 14
January 15 - LUKE 12:32–59, GENESIS 22, PSALM 15
January 16 - LUKE 13:1–17, GENESIS 23, PSALM 16
January 17 - LUKE 13:18–35, GENESIS 24, PSALM 17
January 18 - LUKE 14:1–24, GENESIS 25, PSALM 18
January 19 - LUKE 14:25–35, GENESIS 26, PSALM 19
January 20 - LUKE 15, GENESIS 27:1–45, PSALM 20
January 21 - LUKE 16, GENESIS 27:46–28:22, PSALM 21
January 22 - LUKE 17, GENESIS 29:1–30, PSALM 22
January 23 - LUKE 18:1–17, GENESIS 29:31–30:43, PSALM 23
January 24 - LUKE 18:18–43, GENESIS 31, PSALM 24
January 25 - LUKE 19:1–27, GENESIS 32–33, PSALM 25
January 26 - LUKE 19:28–48, GENESIS 34, PSALM 26
January 27 - LUKE 20:1–26, GENESIS 35–36, PSALM 27
January 28 - LUKE 20:27–47, GENESIS 37, PSALM 28
January 29 - LUKE 21, GENESIS 38, PSALM 29
January 30 - LUKE 22:1–38, GENESIS 39, PSALM 30
January 31 - LUKE 22:39–71, GENESIS 40, PSALM 31

Bible Readings for February

February 1 - LUKE 23:1–25, GENESIS 41, PSALM 32
February 2 - LUKE 23:26–56, GENESIS 42, PSALM 33
February 3 - LUKE 24:1–12, GENESIS 43, PSALM 34
February 4 - LUKE 24:13–53, GENESIS 44, PSALM 35
February 5 - HEBREWS 1, GENESIS 45:1–46:27, PSALM 36
February 6 - HEBREWS 2, GENESIS 46:28–47:31, PSALM 37
February 7 - HEBREWS 3:1–4:13, GENESIS 48, PSALM 38
February 8 - HEBREWS 4:14–6:12, GENESIS 49–50, PSALM 39
February 9 - HEBREWS 6:13–20, EXODUS 1–2, PSALM 40
February 10 - HEBREWS 7, EXODUS 3–4, PSALM 41
February 11 - HEBREWS 8, EXODUS 5:1–6:27, PROVERBS 1
February 12 - HEBREWS 9:1–22, EXODUS 6:28–8:32, PROVERBS 2

February 13 - HEBREWS 9:23–10:18, EXODUS 9–10, PROVERBS 3
February 14 - HEBREWS 10:19–39, EXODUS 11–12, PROVERBS 4
February 15 - HEBREWS 11:1–22, EXODUS 13–14, PROVERBS 5
February 16 - HEBREWS 11:23–40, EXODUS 15, PROVERBS 6:1–7:5
February 17 - HEBREWS 12, EXODUS 16–17, PROVERBS 7:6–27
February 18 - HEBREWS 13, EXODUS 18–19, PROVERBS 8
February 19 - MATTHEW 1, EXODUS 20–21, PROVERBS 9
February 20 - MATTHEW 2, EXODUS 22–23, PROVERBS 10
February 21 - MATTHEW 3, EXODUS 24, PROVERBS 11
February 22 - MATTHEW 4, EXODUS 25–27, PROVERBS 12
February 23 - MATTHEW 5:1–20, EXODUS 28–29, PROVERBS 13
February 24 - MATTHEW 5:21–48, EXODUS 30–32, PROVERBS 14
February 25 - MATTHEW 6:1–18, EXODUS 33–34, PROVERBS 15
February 26 - MATTHEW 6:19–34, EXODUS 35–36, PROVERBS 16
February 27 - MATTHEW 7, EXODUS 37–38, PROVERBS 17
February 28 - MATTHEW 8:1–13, EXODUS 39–40, PROVERBS 18

Bible Readings for March
March 1 - MATTHEW 8:14–34, LEVITICUS 1–2, PROVERBS 19
March 2 - MATTHEW 9:1–17, LEVITICUS 3–4, PROVERBS 20
March 3 - MATTHEW 9:18–38, LEVITICUS 5–6, PROVERBS 21
March 4 - MATTHEW 10:1–25, LEVITICUS 7–8, PROVERBS 22
March 5 - MATTHEW 10:26–42, LEVITICUS 9–10, PROVERBS 23
March 6 - MATTHEW 11:1–19, LEVITICUS 11–12, PROVERBS 24
March 7 - MATTHEW 11:20–30, LEVITICUS 13, PROVERBS 25
March 8 - MATTHEW 12:1–21, LEVITICUS 14, PROVERBS 26
March 9 - MATTHEW 12:22–50, LEVITICUS 15–16, PROVERBS 27
March 10 - MATTHEW 13:1–23, LEVITICUS 17–18, PROVERBS 28
March 11 - MATTHEW 13:24–58, LEVITICUS 19, PROVERBS 29
March 12 - MATTHEW 14:1–21, LEVITICUS 20–21, PROVERBS 30
March 13 - MATTHEW 14:22–36, LEVITICUS 22–23, PROVERBS 31
March 14 - MATTHEW 15:1–20, LEVITICUS 24–25, ECCLESIASTES 1:1–11
March 15 - MATTHEW 15:21–39, LEVITICUS 26–27, ECCLESIASTES 1:12–2:26
March 16 - MATTHEW 16, NUMBERS 1–2, ECCLESIASTES 3:1–15
March 17 - MATTHEW 17, NUMBERS 3–4, ECCLESIASTES 3:16–4:16
March 18 - MATTHEW 18:1–20, NUMBERS 5–6, ECCLESIASTES 5
March 19 - MATTHEW 18:21–35, NUMBERS 7–8, ECCLESIASTES 6
March 20 - MATTHEW 19:1–15, NUMBERS 9–10, ECCLESIASTES 7
March 21 - MATTHEW 19:16–30, NUMBERS 11–12, ECCLESIASTES 8
March 22 - MATTHEW 20:1–16, NUMBERS 13–14, ECCLESIASTES 9:1–12
March 23 - MATTHEW 20:17–34, NUMBERS 15–16, ECCLESIASTES 9:13–10:20
March 24 - MATTHEW 21:1–27, NUMBERS 17–18, ECCLESIASTES 11:1–8
March 25 - MATTHEW 21:28–46, NUMBERS 19–20, ECCLESIASTES 11:9–12:14
March 26 - MATTHEW 22:1–22, NUMBERS 21, SONG OF SOLOMON 1:1–2:7
March 27 - MATTHEW 22:23–46, NUMBERS 22:1–40, SONG OF SOLOMON 2:8-3:5
March 28 - MATTHEW 23:1–12, NUMBERS 22:41–23:26, SONG OF SOLOMON 3:6–5:1

March 29 - MATTHEW 23:13–39, NUMBERS 23:27–24:25,
   SONG OF SOLOMON 5:2–6:3
March 30 - MATTHEW 24:1–31, NUMBERS 25–27, SONG OF SOLOMON 6:4–8:4
March 31 - MATTHEW 24:32–51, NUMBERS 28–29,
   SONG OF SOLOMON 8:5–14

Bible Readings for April
April 1 - MATTHEW 25:1–30, NUMBERS 30–31, JOB 1
April 2 - MATTHEW 25:31–46, NUMBERS 32–34, JOB 2
April 3 - MATTHEW 26:1–25, NUMBERS 35–36, JOB 3
April 4 - MATTHEW 26:26–46, DEUTERONOMY 1–2, JOB 4
April 5 - MATTHEW 26:47–75, DEUTERONOMY 3–4, JOB 5
April 6 - MATTHEW 27:1–31, DEUTERONOMY 5–6, JOB 6
April 7 - MATTHEW 27:32–66, DEUTERONOMY 7–8, JOB 7
April 8 - MATTHEW 28, DEUTERONOMY 9–10, JOB 8
April 9 - ACTS 1, DEUTERONOMY 11–12, JOB 9
April 10 - ACTS 2:1–13, DEUTERONOMY 13–14, JOB 10
April 11 - ACTS 2:14–47, DEUTERONOMY 15–16, JOB 11
April 12 - ACTS 3, DEUTERONOMY 17–18, JOB 12
April 13 - ACTS 4:1–22, DEUTERONOMY 19–20, JOB 13
April 14 - ACTS 4:23–37, DEUTERONOMY 21–22, JOB 14
April 15 - ACTS 5:1–16, DEUTERONOMY 23–24, JOB 15
April 16 - ACTS 5:17–42, DEUTERONOMY 25–27, JOB 16
April 17 - ACTS 6, DEUTERONOMY 28, JOB 17
April 18 - ACTS 7:1–22, DEUTERONOMY 29–30, JOB 18
April 19 - ACTS 7:23–60, DEUTERONOMY 31–32, JOB 19
April 20 - ACTS 8:1–25, DEUTERONOMY 33–34, JOB 20
April 21 - ACTS 8:26–40, JOSHUA 1–2, JOB 21
April 22 - ACTS 9:1–25, JOSHUA 3:1–5:1, JOB 22
April 23 - ACTS 9:26–43, JOSHUA 5:2–6:27, JOB 23
April 24 - ACTS 10:1–33, JOSHUA 7–8, JOB 24
April 25 - ACTS 10:34–48, JOSHUA 9–10, JOB 25
April 26 - ACTS 11:1–18, JOSHUA 11–12, JOB 26
April 27 - ACTS 11:19–30, JOSHUA 13–14, JOB 27
April 28 - ACTS 12, JOSHUA 15–17, JOB 28
April 29 - ACTS 13:1–25, JOSHUA 18–19, JOB 29
April 30 - ACTS 13:26–52, JOSHUA 20–21, JOB 30

Bible Readings for May
May 1 - ACTS 14, JOSHUA 22, JOB 31
May 2 - ACTS 15:1–21, JOSHUA 23–24, JOB 32
May 3 - ACTS 15:22–41, JUDGES 1, JOB 33
May 4 - ACTS 16:1–15, JUDGES 2–3, JOB 34
May 5 - ACTS 16:16–40, JUDGES 4–5, JOB 35
May 6 - ACTS 17:1–15, JUDGES 6, JOB 36
May 7 - ACTS 17:16–34, JUDGES 7–8, JOB 37

May 8 - ACTS 18, JUDGES 9, JOB 38
May 9 - ACTS 19:1–20, JUDGES 10:1–11:33, JOB 39
May 10 - ACTS 19:21–41, JUDGES 11:34–12:15, JOB 40
May 11 - ACTS 20:1–16, JUDGES 13, JOB 41
May 12 - ACTS 20:17–38, JUDGES 14–15, JOB 42
May 13 - ACTS 21:1–36, JUDGES 16, PSALM 42
May 14 - ACTS 21:37–22:29, JUDGES 17–18, PSALM 43
May 15 - ACTS 22:30–23:22, JUDGES 19, PSALM 44
May 16 - ACTS 23:23–24:9, JUDGES 20, PSALM 45
May 17 - ACTS 24:10–27, JUDGES 21, PSALM 46
May 18 - ACTS 25, RUTH 1–2, PSALM 47
May 19 - ACTS 26:1–18, RUTH 3–4, PSALM 48
May 20 - ACTS 26:19–32, 1 SAMUEL 1:1–2:10, PSALM 49
May 21 - ACTS 27:1–12, 1 SAMUEL 2:11–36, PSALM 50
May 22 - ACTS 27:13–44, 1 SAMUEL 3, PSALM 51
May 23 - ACTS 28:1–16, 1 SAMUEL 4–5, PSALM 52
May 24 - ACTS 28:17–31, 1 SAMUEL 6–7, PSALM 53
May 25 - ROMANS 1:1–15, 1 SAMUEL 8, PSALM 54
May 26 - ROMANS 1:16–32, 1 SAMUEL 9:1–10:16, PSALM 55
May 27 - ROMANS 2:1–3:8, 1 SAMUEL 10:17–11:15, PSALM 56
May 28 - ROMANS 3:9–31, 1 SAMUEL 12, PSALM 57
May 29 - ROMANS 4, 1 SAMUEL 13, PSALM 58
May 30 - ROMANS 5, 1 SAMUEL 14, PSALM 59
May 31 - ROMANS 6, 1 SAMUEL 15, PSALM 60

Bible Readings for June

June 1 - ROMANS 7, 1 SAMUEL 16, PSALM 61
June 2 - ROMANS 8, 1 SAMUEL 17:1–54, PSALM 62
June 3 - ROMANS 9:1–29, 1 SAMUEL 17:55–18:30, PSALM 63
June 4 - ROMANS 9:30–10:21, 1 SAMUEL 19, PSALM 64
June 5 - ROMANS 11:1–24, 1 SAMUEL 20, PSALM 65
June 6 - ROMANS 11:25–36, 1 SAMUEL 21–22, PSALM 66
June 7 - ROMANS 12, 1 SAMUEL 23–24, PSALM 67
June 8 - ROMANS 13, 1 SAMUEL 25, PSALM 68
June 9 - ROMANS 14, 1 SAMUEL 26, PSALM 69
June 10 - ROMANS 15:1–13, 1 SAMUEL 27–28, PSALM 70
June 11 - ROMANS 15:14–33, 1 SAMUEL 29–31, PSALM 71
June 12 - ROMANS 16, 2 SAMUEL 1, PSALM 72
June 13 - MARK 1:1–20, 2 SAMUEL 2:1–3:1, DANIEL 1
June 14 - MARK 1:21–45, 2 SAMUEL 3:2–39, DANIEL 2:1–23
June 15 - MARK 2, 2 SAMUEL 4–5, DANIEL 2:24–49
June 16 - MARK 3:1–19, 2 SAMUEL 6, DANIEL 3
June 17 - MARK 3:20–35, 2 SAMUEL 7–8, DANIEL 4
June 18 - MARK 4:1–20, 2 SAMUEL 9–10, DANIEL 5
June 19 - MARK 4:21–41, 2 SAMUEL 11–12, DANIEL 6
June 20 - MARK 5:1–20, 2 SAMUEL 13, DANIEL 7

June 21 - MARK 5:21–43, 2 SAMUEL 14, DANIEL 8
June 22 - MARK 6:1–29, 2 SAMUEL 15, DANIEL 9
June 23 - MARK 6:30–56, 2 SAMUEL 16, DANIEL 10
June 24 - MARK 7:1–13, 2 SAMUEL 17, DANIEL 11:1–19
June 25 - MARK 7:14–37, 2 SAMUEL 18, DANIEL 11:20–45
June 26 - MARK 8:1–21, 2 SAMUEL 19, DANIEL 12
June 27 - MARK 8:22–9:1, 2 SAMUEL 20–21, HOSEA 1:1–2:1
June 28 - MARK 9:2–50, 2 SAMUEL 22, HOSEA 2:2–23
June 29 - MARK 10:1–31, 2 SAMUEL 23, HOSEA 3
June 30 - MARK 10:32–52, 2 SAMUEL 24, HOSEA 4:1–11

Bible Readings for July

July 1 - MARK 11:1–14, 1 KINGS 1, HOSEA 4:12–5:4
July 2 - MARK 11:15–33, 1 KINGS 2, HOSEA 5:5–15
July 3 - MARK 12:1–27, 1 KINGS 3, HOSEA 6:1–7:2
July 4 - MARK 12:28–44, 1 KINGS 4-5, HOSEA 7:3–16
July 5 - MARK 13:1–13, 1 KINGS 6, HOSEA 8
July 6 - MARK 13:14–37, 1 KINGS 7, HOSEA 9:1–16
July 7 - MARK 14:1–31, 1 KINGS 8, HOSEA 9:17–10:15
July 8 - MARK 14:32–72, 1 KINGS 9, HOSEA 11:1–11
July 9 - MARK 15:1–20, 1 KINGS 10, HOSEA 11:12–12:14
July 10 - MARK 15:21–47, 1 KINGS 11, HOSEA 13
July 11 - MARK 16, 1 KINGS 12:1–31, HOSEA 14
July 12 - 1 CORINTHIANS 1:1–17, 1 KINGS 12:32–13:34, JOEL 1
July 13 - 1 CORINTHIANS 1:18–31, 1 KINGS 14, JOEL 2:1–11
July 14 - 1 CORINTHIANS 2, 1 KINGS 15:1–32, JOEL 2:12–32
July 15 - 1 CORINTHIANS 3, 1 KINGS 15:33–16:34, JOEL 3
July 16 - 1 CORINTHIANS 4, 1 KINGS 17, AMOS 1
July 17 - 1 CORINTHIANS 5, 1 KINGS 18, AMOS 2:1–3:2
July 18 - 1 CORINTHIANS 6, 1 KINGS 19, AMOS 3:3–4:3
July 19 - 1 CORINTHIANS 7:1–24, 1 KINGS 20, AMOS 4:4–13
July 20 - 1 CORINTHIANS 7:25–40, 1 KINGS 21, AMOS 5
July 21 - 1 CORINTHIANS 8, 1 KINGS 22, AMOS 6
July 22 - 1 CORINTHIANS 9, 2 KINGS 1–2, AMOS 7
July 23 - 1 CORINTHIANS 10, 2 KINGS 3, AMOS 8
July 24 - 1 CORINTHIANS 11:1–16, 2 KINGS 4, AMOS 9
July 25 - 1 CORINTHIANS 11:17–34, 2 KINGS 5, OBADIAH
July 26 - 1 CORINTHIANS 12, 2 KINGS 6:1–7:2, JONAH 1
July 27 - 1 CORINTHIANS 13, 2 KINGS 7:3–20, JONAH 2
July 28 - 1 CORINTHIANS 14:1–25, 2 KINGS 8, JONAH 3
July 29 - 1 CORINTHIANS 14:26–40, 2 KINGS 9, JONAH 4
July 30 - 1 CORINTHIANS 15:1–34, 2 KINGS 10, MICAH 1
July 31 - 1 CORINTHIANS 15:35–58, 2 KINGS 11, MICAH 2

Bible Readings for August

August 1 - 1 CORINTHIANS 16, 2 KINGS 12–13, MICAH 3
August 2 - 2 CORINTHIANS 1:1–2:4, 2 KINGS 14, MICAH 4
August 3 - 2 CORINTHIANS 2:5–3:18, 2 KINGS 15–16, MICAH 5
August 4 - 2 CORINTHIANS 4:1–5:10, 2 KINGS 17, MICAH 6
August 5 - 2 CORINTHIANS 5:11–6:13, 2 KINGS 18, MICAH 7
August 6 - 2 CORINTHIANS 6:14–7:16, 2 KINGS 19, NAHUM 1
August 7 - 2 CORINTHIANS 8, 2 KINGS 20–21, NAHUM 2
August 8 - 2 CORINTHIANS 9, 2 KINGS 22:1–23:35, NAHUM 3
August 9 - 2 CORINTHIANS 10, 2 KINGS 23:36–24:20, HABAKKUK 1
August 10 - 2 CORINTHIANS 11, 2 KINGS 25, HABAKKUK 2
August 11 - 2 CORINTHIANS 12, 1 CHRONICLES 1–2, HABAKKUK 3
August 12 - 2 CORINTHIANS 13, 1 CHRONICLES 3–4, ZEPHANIAH 1
August 13 - JOHN 1:1–18, 1 CHRONICLES 5–6, ZEPHANIAH 2
August 14 - JOHN 1:19–34, 1 CHRONICLES 7–8, ZEPHANIAH 3
August 15 - JOHN 1:35–51, 1 CHRONICLES 9, HAGGAI 1–2
August 16 - JOHN 2, 1 CHRONICLES 10–11, ZECHARIAH 1
August 17 - JOHN 3:1–21, 1 CHRONICLES 12, ZECHARIAH 2
August 18 - JOHN 3:22–36, 1 CHRONICLES 13–14, ZECHARIAH 3
August 19 - JOHN 4:1–26, 1 CHRONICLES 15:1–16:6, ZECHARIAH 4
August 20 - JOHN 4:27–42, 1 CHRONICLES 16:7–43, ZECHARIAH 5
August 21 - JOHN 4:43–54, 1 CHRONICLES 17, ZECHARIAH 6
August 22 - JOHN 5:1–18, 1 CHRONICLES 18–19, ZECHARIAH 7
August 23 - JOHN 5:19–47, 1 CHRONICLES 20:1–22:1, ZECHARIAH 8
August 24 - JOHN 6:1–21, 1 CHRONICLES 22:2–23:32, ZECHARIAH 9
August 25 - JOHN 6:22–59, 1 CHRONICLES 24, ZECHARIAH 10
August 26 - JOHN 6:60–71, 1 CHRONICLES 25–26, ZECHARIAH 11
August 27 - JOHN 7:1–24, 1 CHRONICLES 27–28, ZECHARIAH 12
August 28 - JOHN 7:25–53, 1 CHRONICLES 29, ZECHARIAH 13
August 29 - JOHN 8:1–20, 2 CHRONICLES 1:1–2:16, ZECHARIAH 14
August 30 - JOHN 8:21–47, 2 CHRONICLES 2:17–5:1, MALACHI 1:1–2:9
August 31 - JOHN 8:48–59, 2 CHRONICLES 5:2–14, MALACHI 2:10–16

Bible Readings for September

September 1 - JOHN 9:1–23, 2 CHRONICLES 6, MALACHI 2:17–3:18
September 2 - JOHN 9:24–41, 2 CHRONICLES 7, MALACHI 4
September 3 - JOHN 10:1–21, 2 CHRONICLES 8, PSALM 73
September 4 - JOHN 10:22–42, 2 CHRONICLES 9, PSALM 74
September 5 - JOHN 11:1–27, 2 CHRONICLES 10–11, PSALM 75
September 6 - JOHN 11:28–57, 2 CHRONICLES 12–13, PSALM 76
September 7 - JOHN 12:1–26, 2 CHRONICLES 14–15, PSALM 77
September 8 - JOHN 12:27–50, 2 CHRONICLES 16–17, PSALM 78:1–20
September 9 - JOHN 13:1–20, 2 CHRONICLES 18, PSALM 78:21–37
September 10 - JOHN 13:21–38, 2 CHRONICLES 19, PSALM 78:38–55
September 11 - JOHN 14:1–14, 2 CHRONICLES 20:1–21:1, PSALM 78:56–72
September 12 - JOHN 14:15–31, 2 CHRONICLES 21:2–22:12, PSALM 79

September 13 - JOHN 15:1–16:4, 2 CHRONICLES 23, PSALM 80
September 14 - JOHN 16:4–33, 2 CHRONICLES 24, PSALM 81
September 15 - JOHN 17, 2 CHRONICLES 25, PSALM 82
September 16 - JOHN 18:1–18, 2 CHRONICLES 26, PSALM 83
September 17 - JOHN 18:19–38, 2 CHRONICLES 27–28, PSALM 84
September 18 - JOHN 18:38–19:16, 2 CHRONICLES 29, PSALM 85
September 19 - JOHN 19:16–42, 2 CHRONICLES 30, PSALM 86
September 20 - JOHN 20:1–18, 2 CHRONICLES 31, PSALM 87
September 21 - JOHN 20:19–31, 2 CHRONICLES 32, PSALM 88
September 22 - JOHN 21, 2 CHRONICLES 33, PSALM 89:1–18
September 23 - 1 JOHN 1, 2 CHRONICLES 34, PSALM 89:19–37
September 24 - 1 JOHN 2, 2 CHRONICLES 35, PSALM 89:38–52
September 25 - 1 JOHN 3, 2 CHRONICLES 36, PSALM 90
September 26 - 1 JOHN 4, EZRA 1–2, PSALM 91
September 27 - 1 JOHN 5, EZRA 3–4, PSALM 92
September 28 - 2 JOHN, EZRA 5–6, PSALM 93
September 29 - 3 JOHN, EZRA 7–8, PSALM 94
September 30 - JUDE, EZRA 9–10, PSALM 95

Bible Readings for October

October 1 - REVELATION 1, NEHEMIAH 1–2, PSALM 96
October 2 - REVELATION 2, NEHEMIAH 3, PSALM 97
October 3 - REVELATION 3, NEHEMIAH 4, PSALM 98
October 4 - REVELATION 4, NEHEMIAH 5:1–7:4, PSALM 99
October 5 - REVELATION 5, NEHEMIAH 7:5–8:12, PSALM 100
October 6 - REVELATION 6, NEHEMIAH 8:13–9:37, PSALM 101
October 7 - REVELATION 7, NEHEMIAH 9:38–10:39, PSALM 102
October 8 - REVELATION 8, NEHEMIAH 11, PSALM 103
October 9 - REVELATION 9, NEHEMIAH 12, PSALM 104:1–23
October 10 - REVELATION 10, NEHEMIAH 13, PSALM 104:24–35
October 11 - REVELATION 11, ESTHER 1, PSALM 105:1–25
October 12 - REVELATION 12, ESTHER 2, PSALM 105:26–45
October 13 - REVELATION 13, ESTHER 3–4, PSALM 106:1–23
October 14 - REVELATION 14, ESTHER 5:1–6:13, PSALM 106:24–48
October 15 - REVELATION 15, ESTHER 6:14–8:17, PSALM 107:1–22
October 16 - REVELATION 16, ESTHER 9–10, PSALM 107:23–43
October 17 - REVELATION 17, ISAIAH 1–2, PSALM 108
October 18 - REVELATION 18, ISAIAH 3–4, PSALM 109:1–19
October 19 - REVELATION 19, ISAIAH 5–6, PSALM 109:20–31
October 20 - REVELATION 20, ISAIAH 7–8, PSALM 110
October 21 - REVELATION 21–22, ISAIAH 9–10, PSALM 111
October 22 - 1 THESSALONIANS 1, ISAIAH 11–13, PSALM 112
October 23 - 1 THESSALONIANS 2:1–16, ISAIAH 14–16, PSALM 113
October 24 - 1 THESSALONIANS 2:17–3:13, ISAIAH 17–19, PSALM 114
October 25 - 1 THESSALONIANS 4, ISAIAH 20–22, PSALM 115
October 26 - 1 THESSALONIANS 5, ISAIAH 23–24, PSALM 116

October 27 - 2 THESSALONIANS 1, ISAIAH 25–26, PSALM 117
October 28 - 2 THESSALONIANS 2, ISAIAH 27–28, PSALM 118
October 29 - 2 THESSALONIANS 3, ISAIAH 29–30, PSALM 119:1–32
October 30 - 1 TIMOTHY 1, ISAIAH 31–33, PSALM 119:33–64
October 31 - 1 TIMOTHY 2, ISAIAH 34–35, PSALM 119:65–96

Bible Readings for November

November 1 - 1 TIMOTHY 3, ISAIAH 36–37, PSALM 119:97–120
November 2 - 1 TIMOTHY 4, ISAIAH 38–39, PSALM 119:121–144
November 3 - 1 TIMOTHY 5:1–22, JEREMIAH 1–2, PSALM 119:145–176
November 4 - 1 TIMOTHY 5:23–6:21, JEREMIAH 3–4, PSALM 120
November 5 - 2 TIMOTHY 1, JEREMIAH 5–6, PSALM 121
November 6 - 2 TIMOTHY 2, JEREMIAH 7–8, PSALM 122
November 7 - 2 TIMOTHY 3, JEREMIAH 9–10, PSALM 123
November 8 - 2 TIMOTHY 4, JEREMIAH 11–12, PSALM 124
November 9 - TITUS 1, JEREMIAH 13–14, PSALM 125
November 10 - TITUS 2, JEREMIAH 15–16, PSALM 126
November 11 - TITUS 3, JEREMIAH 17–18, PSALM 127
November 12 - PHILEMON, JEREMIAH 19–20, PSALM 128
November 13 - JAMES 1, JEREMIAH 21–22, PSALM 129
November 14 - JAMES 2, JEREMIAH 23–24, PSALM 130
November 15 - JAMES 3, JEREMIAH 25–26, PSALM 131
November 16 - JAMES 4, JEREMIAH 27–28, PSALM 132
November 17 - JAMES 5, JEREMIAH 29–30, PSALM 133
November 18 - 1 PETER 1, JEREMIAH 31–32, PSALM 134
November 19 - 1 PETER 2, JEREMIAH 33–34, PSALM 135
November 20 - 1 PETER 3, JEREMIAH 35–36, PSALM 136
November 21 - 1 PETER 4, JEREMIAH 37–38, PSALM 137
November 22 - 1 PETER 5, JEREMIAH 39–40, PSALM 138
November 23 - 2 PETER 1, JEREMIAH 41–42, PSALM 139
November 24 - 2 PETER 2, JEREMIAH 43–44, PSALM 140
November 25 - 2 PETER 3, JEREMIAH 45–46, PSALM 141
November 26 - GALATIANS 1, JEREMIAH 47–48, PSALM 142
November 27 - GALATIANS 2, JEREMIAH 49–50, PSALM 143
November 28 - GALATIANS 3:1–18, JEREMIAH 51–52, PSALM 144
November 29 - GALATIANS 3:19–4:20, LAMENTATIONS 1–2, PSALM 145
November 30 - GALATIANS 4:21–31, LAMENTATIONS 3–4, PSALM 146

Bible Readings for December

December 1 - GALATIANS 5:1–15, LAMENTATIONS 5, PSALM 147
December 2 - GALATIANS 5:16–26, EZEKIEL 1, PSALM 148
December 3 - GALATIANS 6, EZEKIEL 2–3, PSALM 149
December 4 - EPHESIANS 1, EZEKIEL 4–5, PSALM 150
December 5 - EPHESIANS 2, EZEKIEL 6–7, ISAIAH 40
December 6 - EPHESIANS 3, EZEKIEL 8–9, ISAIAH 41
December 7 - EPHESIANS 4:1–16, EZEKIEL 10–11, ISAIAH 42

December 8 - EPHESIANS 4:17–32, EZEKIEL 12–13, ISAIAH 43
December 9 - EPHESIANS 5:1–20, EZEKIEL 14–15, ISAIAH 44
December 10 - EPHESIANS 5:21–33, EZEKIEL 16, ISAIAH 45
December 11 - EPHESIANS 6, EZEKIEL 17, ISAIAH 46
December 12 - PHILIPPIANS 1:1–11, EZEKIEL 18, ISAIAH 47
December 13 - PHILIPPIANS 1:12–30, EZEKIEL 19, ISAIAH 48
December 14 - PHILIPPIANS 2:1–11, EZEKIEL 20, ISAIAH 49
December 15 - PHILIPPIANS 2:12–30, EZEKIEL 21–22, ISAIAH 50
December 16 - PHILIPPIANS 3, EZEKIEL 23, ISAIAH 51
December 17 - PHILIPPIANS 4, EZEKIEL 24, ISAIAH 52
December 18 - COLOSSIANS 1:1–23, EZEKIEL 25–26, ISAIAH 53
December 19 - COLOSSIANS 1:24–2:19, EZEKIEL 27–28, ISAIAH 54
December 20 - COLOSSIANS 2:20–3:17, EZEKIEL 29–30, ISAIAH 55
December 21 - COLOSSIANS 3:18–4:18, EZEKIEL 31–32, ISAIAH 56
December 22 - LUKE 1:1–25, EZEKIEL 33, ISAIAH 57
December 23 - LUKE 1:26–56, EZEKIEL 34, ISAIAH 58
December 24 - LUKE 1:57–80, EZEKIEL 35–36, ISAIAH 59
December 25 - LUKE 2:1–20, EZEKIEL 37, ISAIAH 60
December 26 - LUKE 2:21–52, EZEKIEL 38–39, ISAIAH 61
December 27 - LUKE 3:1–20, EZEKIEL 40–41, ISAIAH 62
December 28 - LUKE 3:21–38, EZEKIEL 42–43, ISAIAH 63
December 29 - LUKE 4:1–30, EZEKIEL 44–45, ISAIAH 64
December 30 - LUKE 4:31–44, EZEKIEL 46–47, ISAIAH 65
December 31 - LUKE 5:1–26, EZEKIEL 48, ISAIAH 66

The way to Jesus Christ is simple:

1. ADMIT THAT YOU ARE A SINNER.

For all have sinned, and come short
of the glory of God.

ROMANS 3:23

2. BELIEVE THAT JESUS IS GOD THE SON WHO PAID THE WAGES OF YOUR SIN.

For the wages of sin is death [eternal separation
from God]; but the gift of God is eternal life
through Jesus Christ our Lord.

ROMANS 6:23

3. CALL UPON GOD.

If thou shalt confess with thy mouth the Lord Jesus,
and shalt believe in thine heart that God hath
raised him from the dead, thou shalt be saved.

ROMANS 10:9

Salvation is a very personal thing between you and God.
The decision is yours alone.